MARKETING STRATEGIES FOR NONPROFIT ORGANIZATIONS

MARKETING STRATEGIES FOR NONPROFIT ORGANIZATIONS

SIRI N. ESPY

LYCEUM
BOOKS, INC

59 E. Van Buren St.
Chicago, IL 60605

To Caitlin, my best creation by far, who has taught me
more than I thought I wanted to know.

©Lyceum Books, Inc. 1993

Published in the United States by
LYCEUM BOOKS, INC.
59 East Van Buren, Ste. 703
Chicago, Illinois 60605

Library of Congress Cataloging-in-Publication Data

Espy, Siri N:
    Marketing strategies for nonprofit organizations / Siri N. Espy,
        p. cm.
    Includes bibliographical references and index.
    ISBN 0-925085-34 X: $19.95
    1. Corporations, Nonprofit—Marketing. I. Title.
HF5415.122.E87   1992
658.8—dc20   91-42063
                                                           CIP

Contents

Preface

Today's nonprofit organizations face a number of challenges and in some cases are turning to business and industry to learn new solutions. Marketing is one concept that nonprofits have "borrowed" from their for-profit counterparts. Many nonprofit organizations, however, are working with an incomplete understanding of the spirit of marketing and struggling with the issue of whether and how to integrate marketing concepts.

Although marketing may sound foreign to mission-driven nonprofits, in fact, it is compatible with their goals and embodies the "nonprofit" values of attention to constituents and the fulfillment of mission. Whether an organization offers comfort or cereal, spiritual values or soap, it can better serve its consumers as well as its own interests if it adopts a marketing orientation as a backdrop to all it does.

This book is intended to demystify marketing for nonprofit organizations, as well as offer practical knowledge to the student and practitioner of nonprofit management. Although the concepts of marketing are not beyond the grasp of even the smallest grassroots organization, marketing does represent a viewpoint, a discipline, and a body of knowledge that must be learned and understood, much like accounting principles or personnel management.

The management of nonprofit organizations is a difficult and often thankless task. Managers often are expected to work long hours to serve complex constituencies for little pay. Those who benefit from the organization's work may demand much and offer little in return. However, many nonprofits have the ability to touch the lives of those they serve in a uniquely meaningful way and to move quickly to fill real, vital needs.

In order for nonprofit organizations to survive and fulfill their altruistic missions, they must begin to understand the realities of the marketplace. Nonprofit managers must become more sophisticated in business administration, and nonprofit boards must learn how to govern in a changing world. Hopefully, the concepts and issues explored in this book will help nonprofit organizations to accomplish these goals.

The process of writing a book is a complex one that begins long before the writer sits at a word processor to compose. A long collection of experiences, both favorable and unfavorable, provide the backdrop for authorship. In this regard, I would like to thank my colleagues at Shadyside Hospital, my clients, and those who have attended my seminars for sharing their successes and frustrations and thereby, providing much of the material for this book. Editor Steve Ott's kind words of encouragement and helpful suggestions also have been greatly appreciated. Last, but not least, my family's patience and understanding have helped me to put one word in front of the other and keep moving.

CHAPTER 1

Nonprofit Marketing: An Overview

The annual meeting of the Youth Wilderness Organization's board of directors is in progress. The executive director concludes her year-end report by recommending that the organization seek new members and work toward providing better experiences for existing participants by initiating a marketing program. "Marketing!" huffs the chairman of the board. "I don't give a hoot for marketing! I never want to see this organization sinking to the level of advertising for members and offering two-for-one coupons to join! For nearly fifty years, we've done a fine job of working with the youth of our community and that's what we'll continue to do."

We all see the effects of marketing every day. It's difficult to imagine a day without billboards, advertising jingles, window displays, and print ads. Our mailboxes are stuffed with "junk," and we are bothered all too often by telemarketers who call at just the wrong time. Christmas displays appear by Halloween, and bathing suits show up in the midst of snowy northern winters in an effort to capture the spirit (and dollars) of the consumer. Corporations spend megabucks attempting to understand and manipulate our psyches, the most personal of all territories. Marketing, we might conclude, is the domain of highly commercialized, profit-oriented industries that attempt to persuade us to buy, buy, buy.

Many nonprofit organizations have resisted the concept of marketing for just this reason. However, there is more to marketing than slick promotion and digging for dollars. Consider the following scenarios:

- A board of directors reviews the organization's mission statement and debates possible future directions
- A zoo director takes members of the donor's club on a special after-hours tour
- A program director at a mental health center sits at her desk compiling statistics on program utilization
- The executive director of a social service agency reviews the results of a client satisfaction survey
- An arts manager reads about a growing national interest in Russian culture
- The receptionist at a medical clinic takes an extra moment to greet an elderly patient and be sure she is comfortable

• The communications committee at a youth center prepares a
brochure listing upcoming activities to mail to parents

What do these seemingly diverse endeavors have in common? They are
all examples of nonprofit marketing in action. So what, then, is marketing, and how can it encompass so many activities?

WHAT IS MARKETING?

Most of us tend to see marketing as a means of selling or promoting
what we have to offer, often to an unwilling audience. However, if done
effectively, marketing is much more than that. Let's look at a working
definition.

Marketing is:

• A means of identifying what is wanted and needed

• A mechanism for bringing an individual or group that has
wants or needs together with an individual or group that can
satisfy those wants or needs

• A focus on understanding and serving the client, customer,
or consumer.

When looked at in these terms, marketing certainly is compatible with
the approach, philosophy, and values of the nonprofit organization.
Even the most humanistic and idealistic among us would agree with the
value of understanding and serving the wants and needs of others. Most
effective marketers do exactly that.

Marketing, then, is a means of bringing the organization together
with donors, referral agents, consumers, other organizations, and important elements of the community as a whole. Without these groups, the
nonprofit is destined to fail. Marketing works with the organization's
mission to allow it to reach out, both getting the resources and giving
the services it is chartered to accomplish.

"Nonprofit" Marketing

"Nonprofit" is a term that causes confusion in many circles. It represents a tax-exempt status and indicates that any excess resources or
profits may not directly benefit or be distributed to the staff, board, or
others in the same manner as a dividend distribution in a for-profit
corporation. Some mistakenly assume that the nonprofit should, at best,
break even each year in the interest of providing good service to its
clientele. In the nonprofit organization, any profit (excess of revenue
over expenses) must remain within the organization, to benefit those it
exists to serve.

In the nonprofit, it is important to remember that doing good is not necessarily in conflict with doing well. A successful nonprofit organization will provide for its own needs in order to be able to continue serving the needs of others. Sound financial management, including building and maintaining a surplus if possible, will allow the nonprofit to ride through the rough times without endangering the entire structure and will permit some risk-taking or loss-producing activities as well.

How do the goals of the nonprofit organization, and therefore, nonprofit marketing, differ from those of the for-profit corporation? In some cases, they are identical, and the definition presented above would be heartily embraced by any corporation. However, there are several important differences in the typical for-profit vs. nonprofit orientation:

• **The for-profit corporation's primary goal is the maximization of shareholder wealth.** Whether the company is a sole proprietorship or shares are owned by individuals who span the globe, the company is successful only if it is profitable. Therefore, in some cases the sole determination of success in the corporation may be the net profit it generates, and more subjective factors, such as serving the clients, could be seen as secondary. It might be argued that net profit is a measure of satisfaction, since consumers vote with their wallets. Although this view is thought to be short-sighted by some people, it is easy to equate a profitable enterprise with a successful one.

• **The nonprofit organization exists to fulfill a particular, well-defined mission.** A quick glance at the annual report of a nonprofit organization will give the reader information about financial success—whether a break even position was achieved or a surplus was generated. This, however, does not in itself measure the success of the nonprofit organization. A food bank, for example, would not be seen as successful if in each successive year more funds flowed into the treasury and fewer dollars were spent. At some point, charges of fraud and misrepresentation might be levied against such an organization. Although financial solvency is certainly vital to the fulfillment of the mission, success also must be measured by how many individuals were served and the effectiveness of that service in producing the desired outcome.

• **Nonprofit organizations must be aware and serve the wants and needs of a multiplicity of stakeholders.** The nonprofit must deal with many groups, such as its board, clients, a network of other service providers, government officials, law enforcement, the educational system, private donors, taxpayers, and many others. Each of these groups may have differing, even conflicting, expectations of the nonprofit organization, yet each group in its own way may be important to the organization's survival.

A few examples will highlight the similarities and differences between nonprofit and for-profit marketing:

• **Creating a demand might be a goal of both.** Television advertising often is geared toward motivating children to nag mom and dad into buying the latest sugar-coated cereal or toward seeking a popular but scarce toy. However, some for-profit corporations have come under fire for attempting to entice minors to drink and smoke through youth-oriented advertising and for exaggerating the benefits of diet aids. Social responsibility and consumerism are fighting back against marketing that seeks to create an unwholesome demand.

Nonprofits also seek to create a demand in some situations: goals such as boosting attendance at a performance, increasing circulation of a publication, or encouraging acceptance of an idea might fit with the organization's mission-defined goals and serve its altruistic purposes. However, there also are limits to which an organization can ethically create a demand. Otherwise, alcoholism treatment facilities and distilleries would team up to encourage the consumption of spirits since that behavior would increase the business of both. In recent years, some nonprofits have come under fire for ethical violations: for example, ad campaigns by hospitals that exaggerate claims of superior technology and seek to disrupt existing doctor–patient relationships and fund-raising appeals that do not portray accurately where the dollar goes.

• **Increasing the financial bottom line is another goal that nonprofits and for-profits share.** The nonprofit is obligated by law to reinvest its surplus in the business, which is the mission of the organization, in contrast to the for-profit corporation whose financial success directly benefits its owners and investors. However, the generation of funds is a worthy goal for any concern. The for-profit business typically earns its revenue through selling products and services, which it targets, provides, and promotes through its marketing efforts. By doing so, it increases earnings and generates additional net revenue for the corporation.

The nonprofit's marketing might be geared toward motivating individuals, corporations, or foundations to donate money, time, or other resources or toward attracting customers to pay for its services. As we've discussed, this approach helps the nonprofit ensure its survival and continued ability to be of service by creating a sound financial position. The organization might seek to bring in "paying customers" or surplus revenue through certain programs in order to subsidize needed but financially unsuccessful services or to allow the provision of services to those who are unable to pay. Marketing as a means of increasing the flow of money into the organization is certainly an honorable and necessary goal.

- **Creating a positive image is a goal that both nonprofit and for-profit organizations share.** The local grocery store wants to be seen as community minded, and the car dealer seeks an honest, fair-dealing reputation. A positive image will encourage customers, which will bring revenue into the business and provide the ultimate measure of success.

Similarly, the nonprofit hopes that its marketing efforts will enhance its image and visibility among donors, clients, and the public in general. The nonprofit hopes that by promoting itself as a provider of a quality product or service it will be successful.

Wants vs. Needs

Throughout this book, we will discuss the role of marketing in determining and satisfying human wants and needs. It is important, therefore, that we define what we mean by these terms.

Wants are different from needs. We can see this in our everyday lives. We need nourishment; we want filet mignon. We need shelter; we want a palatial home with a jacuzzi. Needs are generally inborn and are shared by people around the world. Wants are shaped by our culture and background and are not universal. Some people will seek to satisfy their basic need for food with fried eels, rattlesnake, or dog meat. Others would find this fare unappealing or even repulsive. These distinctions are important in understanding the role of marketing in the nonprofit organization.

Nonprofit organizations exist to satisfy both wants and needs. Some nonprofit organizations serve the homeless, operate food banks, and offer thrift stores to those unable to afford new clothing. They deal with the satisfaction of basic human needs that we all share. Others offer services for the very specific needs of a particular segments of the population, such as medical care for pregnant women or mental health services to schizophrenics. In either case, these activities are widely accepted as essential to the maintenance of a minimum standard of living. Although providers may find funding and service delivery difficult, few would argue that such organizations should not exist.

Many nonprofits serve the wants of society, as well. Libraries satisfy our hunger for knowledge, and the symphony provides us with culture and enjoyment. Youth organizations contribute to the healthy, wholesome development of the next generation, and adoption agencies satisfy longings to nurture and love a child. Although all these organizations might be viewed as essential by those who operate and patronize them, it can be stated with some certainty that human beings have survived without their benefit, in many cases without ill effect. Therefore, these organizations can be thought of as satisfiers of wants.

In our complex and materialistic society, wants tend to greatly outnumber needs and take on an air of pressing importance. Give us food, clothing, shelter, and basic medical care and most of us will survive. However, a simple glance around the room in which you are reading this book will demonstrate how most of us surround ourselves with things that are wanted but really not needed. One could make a case that possession of this book is not a need. We get lost in the distinction between wants and needs in our middle-class certainty that needs will be met and reasonable (and perhaps unreasonable) wishes will be granted.

What we want is not the sole determinant of our behavior. Most of us, if asked, would probably indicate a desire for a Rolls Royce and a trip to a luxury resort. Obviously, reality impinges on the satisfaction of these wants. At times, the simple desire for a hamburger and fries goes unsatisfied because of lack of time, ingredients, or transportation. So the nonprofit must assess the likelihood of these expressed wishes being translated into action, an activity we will discuss when we explore market research.

Marketing the Satisfaction of Wants and Needs

Marketing concepts can and should be applied to the satisfaction of both wants and needs. Even organizations offering the satisfaction of very basic human needs may need to market themselves to potential consumers. It is not safe to assume that everyone seeks to satisfy these needs:

• A mental health clinic serves clients who are depressed, psychotic, and display personality disorders. All of these individuals need assistance through counseling, medication, or institutionalization in order to protect themselves and others or to maximize functioning. However, because of the stigma placed on seeking such services and the distorted perceptions that are part of the initial need, many potential consumers attempt to avoid the very services and organizations that could be of the most benefit.

• Homeless citizens freeze on the streets rather than seek the assistance of shelters because of misunderstanding, suspicion, and reluctance to conform with the rules of "the system." They avoid satisfaction of their basic needs for food and shelter because the means of satisfying those needs conflict with wants, which may seem to hold higher value.

• Low-income pregnant teens fail to take advantage of free prenatal care because of their ignorance of their need for the service as well as a mistrust of the providers. They may endanger their lives and those of their unborn children, although the assistance they need is readily available.

An organization that seeks to satisfy needs by serving clients such as those mentioned above must assume the complex task of understanding and meeting the consumer on terms acceptable to both parties. This can improve relationships with other service providers, law enforcement agencies, and the community as a whole. The organization may seek the assistance of families and significant persons in the lives of potential clients. It may provide additional information and supportive, easy means of entry. These functions might be classified as outreach activities, but they clearly are within the domain of marketing—seeking to understand and satisfy human wants and needs in a user-friendly manner that will encourage the consumer to make or accept the initial contact and keep coming back.

The need to apply marketing principles to the want-oriented organization is more obvious. First, the organization must assess whether the want exists or can be created:

- Does a rural community with high poverty levels really want a performing arts center and will it support one?
- Can a new upscale nursing home compete with several more affordable, well-established facilities that are never at capacity?
- Will a children's museum succeed in a community with a high average age and declining population?

The organization must assess whether the target groups want the proposed service. This exercise may scrub the idea in the incubation stage. In addition, the organization must determine whether the want is strong enough to support its activities and to sustain its existence over the long haul.

Many nonprofits conduct "needs assessments," which might be thought of as part of the marketing process in the terms described above. Again, the focus is on determining the needs of the population to be served before making decisions about the allocation of scarce resources and on assuring that the programs will be well utilized. Unfortunately, such assessments sometimes are completed for political reasons or to support decisions that have already been made—a problem inherent in any decision-making process.

Marketing, then, determines what human wants and needs might be and how best to match resources with what constituents are likely to use and from what they will benefit. This clearly is not an easy process; people are complex beings. To be effective, the marketer needs to be able to play psychologist to a wide variety of people.

Marketing as Mission

Nonprofit organizations, on the whole, have evolved from a sense of purpose and mission and the desire to fulfill human wants and/or needs. Presumably, the motivation for founding the nonprofit organization is not related directly to personal economic benefit, because nonprofits are prohibited from dispensing excess revenue to individuals. The nonprofit, then, typically serves a specific group or type of individual. In order to do this effectively, the organization's board and staff adopt a mission statement that conveys to the reader why that organization exists and what it has set out to do, such as:

> Mother Love Daycare Center provides affordable care to the children of low-income parents in a Christian atmosphere. Our goal is to break the poverty cycle by allowing parents to pursue employment or educational activities while we provide children with nourishing meals, security, and educational and emotional enrichment.

Let's think about the laudable mission of Mother Love Daycare Center and look at our definition of marketing. How does the concept of marketing fit?

First, marketing is a means of identifying what is wanted and needed. Prior to the startup of the center, the founders researched the problems of the community and found that there was a need. By looking at local demographics, it was determined that there are a significant number of low-income families in the area. By interviewing child development specialists at the community schools, the founders learned that many children from these families reach school age lacking proper nutrition and educational and social skills. Local social service agencies that had worked with these parents offered the information that many felt unable to look for jobs or return to school because they were unable to afford child care and often extended families were not in the area. After doing some additional research, the founders felt certain that the center was what these parents wanted and needed.

Second, marketing is a mechanism for bringing an individual or group that has wants or needs together with an individual or group that can satisfy those wants or needs. After the founders of Mother Love Daycare Center secured funding and decided to open for business, they were faced with the problem of bringing these in need (low-income parents) together with those who could satisfy their needs (the center). Wisely, they knew that simply because there is a need potential consumers will not flock automatically to a potential source of satisfaction. Mother Love had to get the word out, overcome suspicion, and help parents to feel that their children would be cared for. To do this, they developed a promotional plan that involved local community leaders, social service agencies, and personal contacts in the community. Slowly, parents began using the center, and it eventually reached full utilization.

Third, marketing represents a focus on understanding and serving the client, customer, or consumer. The board and staff of the Center were aware that in order to fulfill their mission, they must monitor continually the level of customer satisfaction and seek new ways to serve. To accomplish this, they periodically invite groups of parents to meet with them and provide input and feedback. They have formed a parents' advisory board and are in touch with officials at the school as well as social service agencies. Out of these discussions, new programs have developed and the director can deal with problems before they become crises. Mother Love Daycare Center would be incapable of fulfilling its mission if it did not adequately research the needs of the community, work to bring in potential clients, and continue to satisfy their needs.

This example is intended to illustrate two major points:

- Marketing is not simply promoting the service once it is in place; it is an integrated approach to management and planning.
- Marketing is a vital part of any organization's success in fulfilling its mission and reaching those whom it exists to serve.

Marketing vs. Selling

Imagine, for a moment, that you are a marketing executive for an ice cream manufacturer. Your company has decided to add another flavor to its product line—garlic ice cream. You think of yourself as a crack marketer, so you go to work lining up the hottest celebrities to promote your new product. You spend millions on prime time TV advertising, print ads, and billboards and place coupons in all the major newspapers and family magazines. You have done everything by the book and have come up with what should be an award-winning advertising campaign. But surprise! The product is a dismal failure, is discontinued quickly, and you are pounding the pavement resume in hand.

It doesn't take a marketing wizard to determine what went wrong. The ice cream company did an excellent job of trying to sell a product that no one wanted to buy. The moral of the story is that effective marketing is much more than just selling a product. It is a way of thinking about doing business that focuses, from the beginning, on determining and serving wants and needs.

Let's look at the difference between marketing and selling:

- Marketing is a consumer-based activity designed to allow you to identify actual and potential customers; assess their needs, attitudes, and preferences; and plan to serve their wants and needs. It is aimed at filling the needs of consumers by offering them products, programs, or services that they will find attractive, beneficial, and useful.

• Selling is an organization-based activity aimed at motivating others to consume what your organization has to offer. It is geared toward filling the needs of the organization by selling programs and services in order to ensure survival and profitability.

If we flash back to our original working definition of marketing, we see that selling is only one part of the process of bringing people with wants and needs together with a potential satisfier of those wants and needs. Selling comes near the end of a lengthy marketing process that begins with an idea and includes the research that must be done to ensure that the idea is a marketable one.

Unfortunately, many nonprofits have had their own experiences of selling garlic ice cream:

- A senior activity center was located in a site that required a long walk from the bus and up a steep hill.

- A mental health facility opened a satellite in a community where many residents felt it was poor judgment to air one's dirty laundry with strangers.

- An adult daycare center attempted to provide its services in an ethnic area where residents believed it was the responsibility of daughters and daughters-in-law to care for the elderly at home.

- An AIDS support program sought to reach heterosexuals at risk but was perceived as being operated by and for the gay community.

In each of these cases, the original idea may have been an excellent one (far superior to garlic ice cream), but the organization's efforts to sell the idea were doomed to failure because of a lack of solid, up-front marketing. In each of these cases, potential consumers simply were unwilling to "buy" a service that they did not feel would meet their wants or needs. An organization that does not pinpoint effectively those wants and needs and how to satisfy them has failed from the beginning; any additional efforts to proceed with planning and marketing the program are highly unlikely to succeed.

Attitudes Toward Nonprofit Marketing

As in the for-profit sector, the outward evidence of nonprofit marketing is inescapable. Nonprofits use direct mail communications, billboards, print ads, telemarketing, radio, and television just as their for-profit counterparts. Larger nonprofits have marketing departments, and even smaller nonprofit organizations are scrambling to hire a "marketing person."

Attitudes toward nonprofit marketing vary widely. The concept of marketing has become trendy in some circles, with the addition of a marketing function seen as a panacea for the organization's ills. At the other extreme, some nonprofit managers and board members find the idea of marketing for nonprofit organizations superfluous at best and crass and offensive at worst. Let's examine these opposing attitudes and the pitfalls of each:

Marketing as a Quick Fix.   Managers always are seeking ways to improve the operation of the organization. Unfortunately, in some cases they fail to do their homework and in the zeal for a quick fix, reach for unrealistic solutions. Marketing often falls into the category of being a quick fix. An organization with problems in utilization, visibility, or funding might seek to "hire someone" to improve the situation. All too often this solution is poorly thought out, and the individual hired faces an impossible task. Consider the following scenario:

> An organization dealing with emotionally disturbed children has pro-
> liferated rapidly over the past few years. It has sought and received
> funding for many new programs, and its budget has tripled as a
> result. New staff members have been hired for each program, and
> the executive director who had competently presided over a small
> grassroots organization now lacks the skills to lead a complex, multi-
> faceted agency. The organization is falling into disarray, the staff lacks
> direction, and the clients are dissatisfied. Some of the new programs
> are poorly organized and have not been well received. The director
> and board review the utilization statistics of the many scattered pro-
> grams, listen to the grumblings of a disenchanted constituency, and
> feel great relief when they make a forward-thinking decision: hire a
> marketing person.

Unfortunately, this drama is acted out often in nonprofit boardrooms. The organization recruits a competent, well-meaning marketer who tries—and fails—to reach the ill-defined goals of "getting us some visibility" or "improving our numbers." This organization and many others like it are committing the sins discussed above—mistaking selling for marketing and seeing good marketing as a substitute for good management. This story might have several sad endings:

• The marketing person struggles against the tide and attempts to work with the public, but temporary flashes of success and brilliance are followed with more dissatisfaction when the organization fails to deliver the promised goods. Growing weary of the fight, the marketer becomes as ineffective as the rest of the organization.

• The marketer, being a sharp and perceptive individual, develops a marketing plan, works with the staff and board, and makes appropriate outside contacts. Acquiring sound skills and a positive reputation, the marketer moves on to an organization better able to utilize these skills in a true marketing orientation.

• Unaware of the writing on the wall, the marketer becomes a scapegoat. After failing to accomplish the unrealistic goals and solve organizational problems several levels up, the individual is fired. Board and management express their disappointment in "such a promising person."

Marketing Just Doesn't Fit Here.   At the other end of the spectrum, many nonprofits have been slow to adopt the principles and functions of sound marketing. Many reasons are given by nonprofit managers for ignoring the entire idea:

• A nonprofit organization doesn't need to do marketing.
• It can't be done within the typical nonprofit budget.
• Our staff already is too busy.
• If you have a good product or service, it will sell itself.
• We already have a good reputation in the community—what more do we need?
• We've been doing fine without marketing for all these years— you can't argue with success.

These statements all reflect a fundamental misunderstanding of the function and benefits of a marketing approach. Marketing doesn't require a department or even a budget; again, it is an approach to understanding and serving the wants and needs of the individuals or groups the organization exists to serve. Ideally, a marketing approach is something that can become a part of all of the organization's activities rather than a separate function that performs mystical acts to achieve magical results.

There is little doubt that an organization that fails to adapt to today's competitive environment may have great difficulty in gaining the visibility, clients, funding, and community support it needs to survive and prosper. Organizations that rely on past success and fail to use the best possible approach to planning for the future will probably find themselves falling behind their competitors.

Many nonprofit managers fear that they lack the skills and vision to carry forth an effective marketing program, and in some cases they are correct. Although it can be done without a megabudget, marketing does represent a body of knowledge and a set of skills that generally are not instinctive and inborn. Competent managers may have a lot to learn before attempting to "marketize" their organizations.

Subsequent chapters will discuss various facets of marketing and how marketing can be used effectively in the nonprofit. The bottom line is that marketing techniques and approaches can be adapted for use by even the smallest organization. It is possible to develop a truly market-driven organization according to the definition presented above with little or no additional expenditure by integrating marketing principles into existing activities with existing staff. Attention to matching wants and needs with the organization's offerings and reaching out to consumers and ensuring their satisfaction is simply good business sense for any organization.

BENEFITS TO THE CONSUMER AND THE ORGANIZATION

Why should the nonprofit organization worry about marketing? Most nonprofits are on extremely limited budgets, with little cash or staff time to spare. Many have all the clients they need, and some are guaranteed funding through reliable (or at least governmental) sources. Many organizations may have survived for many years without an organized marketing function and may wonder why they should start now.

Marketing is becoming, in some nonprofit circles, trendy—the latest buzzword. Nonprofits are discovering a phenomenon that has been around for many years in for-profit circles, and suddenly marketing is a hot topic. There are, however, many concrete, measurable benefits to developing and implementing a sound marketing program. Again, let's flash back to our definition of marketing and show how its application will benefit both the organization and the consumer. **Marketing is a means of identifying what is wanted and needed.**

Organizational Benefits

Knowing what is wanted and needed by the consumer is an important ingredient in the organization's eventual success. Without a firm grasp of what is likely to be accepted, the organization might devote scarce resources to superfluous or poorly utilized programs. Success in the marketplace, whether that is defined as customers, donors, or the community in general, depends on the organization's ability to identify what is wanted and needed and therefore, what will "sell."

Consumer Benefits

Every day, we are at the mercy of organizations that serve us badly. Stores fail to carry the items we want, doctors force us to endure unreasonable waits, and repairs are never done on time. It is refreshing, even miraculous, to discover an organization that truly seems interested in providing good service, even anticipating our wants and needs. The result is a loyal public, satisfied customers, and a successful business. A nonprofit that applies marketing principles to successfully identify and provide what clients seek will better serve its constituents, who will feel themselves the better for having associated with the organization. **Marketing is a mechanism for bringing together an individual or group that has wants or needs with an individual or group that can satisfy those wants or needs.**

Organizational Benefits

As illustrated in the examples of the homeless person and the pregnant teen, an organization's effectiveness depends on the ability to reach those it seeks to serve. Whether the organization attempts to reach indigent clients or wealthy donors, the appeal must fit the audience and be presented in a manner that will produce the desired response. A marketing approach will allow the organization to effectively bring its wares to the target market. An organization that is not effective in reaching those it is in business to serve will not survive long; fees for service will be inadequate to meet needs, and donors and other funders will be uninterested in meeting the needs of those organizations that are not meeting the needs of their constituents.

Consumer Benefits

Many of us spend inordinate amounts of time looking for the products and services that will satisfy our desires. Who among us has not made fruitless searches for that one item that will bring satisfaction? The clientele of nonprofit organizations can include people with special needs that may impair their ability to effectively search for the appropriate service and provider. Even those of us with "normal" capacity may not know where to seek fulfillment of our wishes for just the right music to soothe our souls or an organization to meet our social needs.

Nonprofit marketing informs us of the products and services provided. Although it may be obvious that clothing can be found in a department store and food in a grocery store, many nonprofit goods and services tend to be complex and well hidden, and potential consumers are unaware of their existence and availability. Marketing serves as a means for providing information and encouragement to the public. Marketing provides an outreach to potential consumers, who can enjoy maximum benefit from the nonprofit's good work. **Marketing focuses on understanding and serving the client, customer, or consumer.**

Organizational Benefits

The organization that effectively serves its consumers is most likely to enjoy a long and happy life. Important groups such as donors, referral groups, and direct consumers are essential to the organization's ultimate survival. A solid understanding of the wants and needs of the consumer will provide the basis for building an organization with a positive reputation as well as effective fulfillment of its mission.

Consumer Benefits

Many organizations take their best guess at the needs of their constituents. It is easy to make ivory tower judgments about the best interests of those individuals and just as easy to miss the mark. In this case, the consumer finds an abundance of products and services that do not meet genuine wants and needs, and few that do. There is little to be gained by involvement with an organization that fails to attend to and serve actual needs.

WHAT DO NONPROFITS MARKET?

Nonprofit organizations, as we have discussed, have specific, well-defined missions that tell us why they exist and what they intend to accomplish. Early in their existence and throughout the stages of their development, the organization must decide what it will provide to its target groups. Nonprofits typically market one or more of the following:

- Services
- Experiences
- Products
- Concepts
- The organization

In order to understand how nonprofits effectively market their wares, let's look at each category and how marketing fits in:

Services

For many nonprofit organizations, providing services is a vital part of their mission. These might include medical services, support groups, spaying and neutering pets, legal assistance, and job placement. In each case, clients come to the organization to satisfy a want or need through a service, which typically is intangible, provided by the organization. In many cases, it is impossible to see, and therefore difficult to understand, a service.

Many clients seeking services are unsure what to expect or what they should receive:

• A recently divorced middle-aged woman makes an appointment for counseling at a family service agency. She talks to the therapist for an hour, then demands to know what she should do about her ex-husband and the "cheap mistress" he intends to marry. When the therapist fails to make specific recommendations or decisions for the client, she becomes angry and never returns.

• An elderly woman visits an arthritis clinic expecting that she will leave with medication that will cure her problem. She is disgusted and disappointed with the advice of the physician at the clinic and tells her friends at the senior center that "those doctors don't know what they're doing."

In both cases, the providers are dealing with the pitfalls inherent in the service delivery process. At times, the customer is the product. The organization takes the client from an initial point in an initial state and through its intervention turns out the client at the end of the process, presumably in improved condition. The changes may be obvious, as in the case of a facelift at an ambulatory surgery center, or invisible, as in the outcome of credit counseling. The outcome of the services may be unsuccessful despite the organization's best efforts and doing everything "right"—a hospital emergency room is unable to save the lives of all those brought in and clients of a women's shelter can't always be protected from abuse.

The nonprofit organization planning to market a service faces a number of pitfalls and challenges, as indicated above. Building and clarifying expectations, then meeting them satisfactorily is not an easy task. However, there also is great potential for a satisfied customer and a positive impact on the organization, the individual, and society.

Experiences

Some nonprofit organizations specialize in experiences. Experiences are perhaps the ultimate in intangibles, but one might argue that our experiences are what makes our lives richer and stand between drudgery and enlightenment. Experiences provided by these nonprofits include a visit to the museum, musical and dramatic performances, gym classes for toddlers, and educational excursions to Europe. Although in some cases these things might be thought of as services, experiences tend to take us above the mundane and essential elements of life and enhance our enjoyment. They satisfy our wants rather than our needs. None of the items mentioned above are vital to our physical survival, although some might champion their importance to the soul.

A nonprofit that specializes in experiences faces the task of convincing potential consumers that this specific experience is worthy of their time and money. In a major city where experience-oriented nonprofits cluster, there often is an abundance of competing experiences; for example, various performances, exhibits, and shows compete for the cultural dollar. Again, we must invoke our concept of marketing—discovering what the consumer seeks, bringing the offering to the appropriate audience, and ensuring the customer's satisfaction, which will increase the likelihood of organizational success.

Products

Some nonprofits offer products—tangible, actual goods. Some examples:

- The family planning clinic offers birth control devices for sale to clients.
- The museum sells books on topics such as art and natural history, as well as toy dinosaurs and reproductions of works of art.
- A child abuse prevention agency offers free literature on signs of parental stress and effective childrearing.
- The animal shelter sells pet supplies, books on animal care, and takes your pet's picture with Santa for a fee.
- The nature center sells birdseed, feeders, and books on identifying and watching wild animals.
- An organization devoted to safety provides brochures and booklets on accident-proofing your home.
- A disease-related organization auctions items donated by celebrities.
- A youth organization sells cookies and candy to the public.

The above list shows the variety of products nonprofits offer. Products can be offered for several major reasons:

- To fulfill the mission of the organization.
- To raise funds to bring the organization additional resources with which to fulfill its mission.

Birdseed, birth control, and safety brochures are all mission related. These items directly relate to the reason the organization exists, and their distribution helps the organization to reach its stated goals.

Having an auction that offers celebrity items and selling cookies and candy are not directly related to the organizations' missions; these organizations do not exist to further celebrity recognition or increase sugar consumption. These products are offered by the organization primarily for fund-raising purposes, although free publicity and public awareness may be a welcome benefit.

There are some products that serve a dual purpose—the nature society may sell birdseed at a significant markup in order to enhance its treasury as well as the welfare of the feathered consumers. The picture of Rover with Santa heightens animals awareness, fosters positive emotions, and brings needed revenue into the shelter.

The marketer's task with selling nonprofit products is similar to that of the for-profit marketer who focuses on consumer goods, but there often is a twist. In many cases, we can buy cookies for less at the grocery store, and the local discount mart may offer a bargain on pet leashes. We are selling a cause as well as a consumable item; we are providing an opportunity for philanthropy as well as a purchase. Philanthropy can make the job easier, but consumers who consider their own bank account the ultimate charity may resist buying the product.

Concepts

Many nonprofit organizations are in the business of selling concepts or ideas. Some concepts might include:

- Say no to drugs.
- Stop smoking for the sake of your health.
- Guarantee a woman's right to a safe, legal abortion.
- Outlaw the killing of unborn babies.
- Don't wear fur; it represents cruelty to animals.
- Read to your children.
- Outlaw handguns.
- Protect America's right to bear arms.
- Don't drink and drive.
- Attend the church or synagogue of your choice.

Organizations that put out such messages typically do so in fulfillment of their mission. Unlike some types of marketing, the goals of such communication often do not include gaining direct customers for the organization or increasing revenue. In this sense, nonprofits hold the rather unique position of attempting to market concepts that will yield no direct benefit to the organization other than the fulfillment of mission.

Although some organizations may provide assistance in carrying out their suggestion (contact us for information on smoking cessation; write for a free pamphlet on knowing when you've drunk too much to drive), in many cases the organization does not expect to have any direct contact with those it reaches through its informational campaign. The communication is successful if it educates, informs, and persuades.

Organizations that seek to sell ideas such as those mentioned above face the challenge of establishing what types of people to target, what type of appeal will be effective, and how to measure the outcome. Unlike a museum that can count attendance or a crisis hotline that can track callers, the sellers of concepts can have a much more difficult marketing task.

Attempting to impact people through the marketing of concepts can be a difficult challenge, calling for sophisticated strategies and evaluation research. In order to determine what types of appeals are effective and gauge the outcome of efforts, nonprofits need to face the challenge of gathering information on attitude and behavior change in people with whom they may otherwise have no direct contact. Although this can be a difficult and costly task, the alternative is proceeding without feedback, which can prove costly because of the waste of resources targeted for the accomplishment of an intangible, ill-defined goal.

The marketing of such ideas and concepts, also known as **social marketing**, requires an understanding of the people the organization seeks to reach. For example, if the ultimate goal of an organization is the elimination of smoking, such a broad goal may require specific, targeted strategies. A campaign to prevent smoking in teenagers might be targeted through the school system and include appeals by the latest teen idols who indicate that smoking is not a fashionable thing to do. Such an approach would be inappropriate in reaching middle-aged persons with early indications of lung disease who might well be reached through information provided by physicians appealing to concerns about health and longevity. Identification of all the various segments of society who smoke, mechanisms for reaching them, and differences in targeting the appeal will illustrate the difficulty in launching a far-reaching effort to market ideas. Similar to other types of marketing, the marketer must realize that unless the appeal is tied to something the receiver of the communication of wants or needs (such as being fashionable or healthy) it is likely to be ineffective.

The rather nebulous nature of social marketing calls for attention to the effectiveness of the message. The marketer ideally should research the characteristics, perceptions, and motivations of the groups targeted. It is important to know which messages will "hook" the audience and which seem irrelevant or uninteresting. Likewise, the organization needs to understand how and whether the idea will translate into the desired behavior. For example, the goal of a smoking cessation campaign is not merely to convince the public that smoking is a bad idea—even hard-core smokers tend to agree that it is. Taking attitudinal factors a step further and changing behavior is an additional and complex step. Remembering that the nonprofit is unlikely to make direct contact with those targeted in the campaign illustrates the complexity of this marketing task.

The Organization

In some organizations, a major goal is marketing itself. Political parties, professional societies, and churches might be a few examples. Such organizations recruit members. They may offer services, products, experiences, and concepts, but ultimately they will survive by persuading people to join and offer their financial support, membership statistics, volunteer hours, votes, and other benefits.

In the case of this sort of organization, the marketing task involves determining who the potential joiner is, how this type of individual is to be reached, and what benefits will be of sufficient appeal to achieve the desired membership.

> Churches, some of which have suffered a decline in membership, offer nurseries for young children, activities for couples, and their facilities to community groups, preschools, or daycare centers during the week. Some churches even advertise in the mass media or launch direct mail campaigns to the local area. Although all these activities are related to the church's mission, they also are good marketing. The activities are based on an assessment of the community's wants and needs and are done in an effort to bring the potential churchgoer to the church and create a satisfied customer who will continue membership, attendance, financial support, volunteer work, and will in turn recruit additional members by recommending the church or bringing a friend. In this way, the church can survive and carry its spiritual message to a wider circle of believers.

THE FOUR PS IN NONPROFIT MARKETING

Marketing pundits identify four primary facets of the marketer's job—price, product, place, and promotion—and interestingly they all begin with the letter "p." Although these concepts were developed primarily for application in traditional, for-profit organizations, let's examine each in the context of the marketing tasks of the nonprofit organization.

Price

Cost can be an important consideration for nonprofits. Although consumers may have once been oblivious to the cost of healthcare, some now shop around for the best price on prescriptions or procedures or for the doctor who will accept insurance as full payment for services. Low cost is important to some consumers, as in lower-income families needing sliding scale counseling fees or an affordable retirement center. On the other end of the scale, inexpensive counseling fees and entrance fees to a retirement village may signal low-class, low-quality, undesirable services to those who seek the best and are willing and able to pay a premium.

The nonprofit, then, must set its prices to correspond to the wants and needs of those it seeks to serve to the fullest extent possible, keeping in mind the funding realities the organization faces. An arts organization with a primarily well-to-do clientele and well-attended functions would be unlikely to drop prices. However, the zoo may seek to keep entrance fees affordable and offer special rates to children and seniors to appeal to a mass audience. Prices that are too high or too low can be a deterrent to the organization's ability to reach out and fulfill its mission.

Prices also can be nonmonetary when the concept is applied broadly. Some organizations seek a commitment of volunteer service from their members or require a lifestyle commitment, such as abstinence from drinking or violent behavior. These costs of involvement in a nonprofit organization also must be considered. Setting the "price" too low may impede the organization's ability to reach its goals, but requiring too large a commitment may limit severely those who are willing or able to become involved with the organization.

Products

As we discussed above, products are not always the tangible goods we might imagine. Except for the fact that it does not begin with "p," we might think of the "offerings" rather than the "products" of nonprofits. In any case, it is incumbent upon the organization to offer an appealing mix of products, services, experiences, and concepts as well as examine the marketability of the organization itself. A nonprofit that does not attend to wants and needs faces a dreary future.

Place

This refers to where and how the nonprofit actually offers its wares. Determining how and where the offerings of the nonprofit might best be utilized is an important focus for the organization as it seeks to reach its goal through marketing. The senior center that was located on top of a steep hill was not attending to the needs of its potential clientele. A recreation center serving delinquent, low-income youths might find that a space adjacent to the police station, however attractive and otherwise suitable, might deter attendance. The nonprofit, then, must seek to locate and "sell" its offerings in a manner that will be perceived as safe, attractive, and appealing—subjective judgments that will differ depending on the audience the organization seeks to reach.

Promotion

This is the concept that many of us erroneously equate with marketing. Although it is only one facet of the marketing process, it is a vital one—it represents the noise the tree makes when it falls in the forest. Without appropriate promotion, even well-conceived, potentially useful, and attractive offerings may fail. A part of any well-planned marketing effort is the determination of how the organization will bring its endeavors to the awareness of those who might benefit.

DEVELOPING A MARKETING ORIENTATION

Effective nonprofit organizations tend to view marketing as a total, integrated approach rather than an isolated activity conducted by a specific individual or department. We might think of these activities as elements of a marketing orientation:

- Conducting program activities with an eye to what the clients want or need.
- Paying attention to the user-friendliness of everything we do.
- Placing customer or client satisfaction as one of our most important values.
- Running frequent checks on operations to be certain that we are achieving our goals.
- Compiling and using available information about the organization in program and service planning and evaluation.
- Keeping track of changes in the community, state, nation, or world that might impact the way we do business.
- Providing information and ongoing education to the staff on the value of a marketing, customer-centered approach.

Too many times, unfortunately, organizations can become overly enamored of their skills and expertise. After all, the staff may have advanced degrees and considerable experience in their field of endeavor. That means that they make the best decisions about what their constituents want and need, right?

The development of a marketing orientation means that organizational decisions are not exclusively the domain of those with the credentials to make them. The customers may not always be right, but they may have some very good ideas. Marketing-oriented organizations seek to understand and fill the wants and needs of the customer, quirky though they may be. Of course, there may be limits on the organization's ability to accomplish that goal—the budget may not allow or professional judgment might prohibit increasing consumer pleasure by, say, including a glass of wine with meals in an alcoholism treatment facility. However, there is always value in seeking and utilizing the opinions of those you exist to serve.

Many of us have been attracted to a product or company because of appealing and effective promotional efforts, only to discover that the hype was far more compelling than what was delivered. In this case, the organization has fallen short of developing a true marketing orientation. By focusing on promotion, only part of the marketing job has been accomplished. The organization has failed to understand the consumer's wants and needs and to work toward their satisfaction. Although there may be a ground swell of interest resulting from a clever promotional campaign, effective marketing not only attracts customers and makes the initial sale, it works toward building relationships that will last beyond the first contact.

WHERE DO WE GO FROM HERE?

Earlier in this chapter, a number of scenarios were presented representing nonprofit marketing in action. They gave us some examples of how the marketing process applies to nonprofits in various settings. Each of the following activities represents a facet of marketing and a major topic to be examined in this book:

- **A Board of Directors reviews the organization's mission statement and debates possible future directions.** This activity represents strategic planning, a fundamental activity that should form the basis of any organization's marketing efforts. Chapter 2 will address the role, importance, and method of strategic planning in the nonprofit.

- **A zoo director takes members of the donor's club on a special after-hours tour.** Nonprofit marketing, as explained in chapter 3, focuses on knowing and understanding the customer, a broad definition that includes the tasks of pleasing donors, consumers, volunteers, and other groups.

- **A program director at a mental health center sits at her desk, compiling statistics on program utilization.** A fundamental marketing task is building awareness of trends both within and outside the organization that will impact the way it will do business. Chapter 4 will examine these internal and external analyses in marketing.

The executive director of a social service agency reviews the results of a client satisfaction survey. Market research, explored in chapter 5, is a method of keeping on top of the changing market of nonprofit offerings. It provides valuable information that can help to accurately target marketing efforts.

An arts manager reads about a growing interest in Russian culture. Evaluating products and services and becoming a market-driven organization are the topics in chapter 6. Nonprofits must always look for opportunities to bring new ideas to the marketplace, serve the consumer, and enrich the organization.

The receptionist at a medical clinic takes an extra moment to greet an elderly patient and be sure she is comfortable. As we will explore in chapter 7, there are many facets to the nonprofit marketing program. The entire staff can become marketers, carrying out a marketing plan and its goals and objectives.

The communications committee at a youth center prepares a brochure listing upcoming activities to mail to parents. The marketing communications or promotion function, presented in chapter 8, addresses the need to disseminate information about the organization's offerings. It represents one step in a multifaceted marketing program.

REVIEW QUESTIONS

1. What is marketing? How does it differ from selling?
2. What are some major similarities and differences in the goals and marketing tasks of nonprofit vs. for-profit organizations?
3. What are wants and needs, and how does the nonprofit address each?
4. How does marketing help the nonprofit fulfill its mission?
5. What are the pitfalls associated with resistance to marketing in the nonprofit on one extreme and seeing it as a cure-all on the other?
6. What do we mean by developing a marketing orientation? Why is this important?
7. What are the major benefits to the consumer and the organization of applying marketing principles to activities?
8. What do nonprofits typically market? What are some of the challenges faced in each case?
9. What are the four Ps of nonprofit marketing? Why is each important?
10. How would you respond to a nonprofit manager who stated, "We don't need a marketing program here—we've been successful in what we do for thirty years!"?

MINI CASE STUDY

The Children's Center is a nonprofit adoption agency that has existed for twenty years and provides a number of services:

- Counseling for pregnant women who are considering placing the baby for adoption
- Counseling for infertile couples
- Studies of prospective adoptive parents to determine their suitability and the type of child they should receive
- Matching and placement of available children with adoptive families
- Support and evaluation services until the adoption is finalized
- Follow-up counseling for the child and family should there be a need

The Children's Center struggles with the same problems as other adoption programs. Most of the couples seeking their services are interested in a "healthy white infant," although a high abortion rate and greater acceptance of "unwed motherhood" has reduced the number of available children fitting that description. Most of the children waiting for placement are of minority races, older, handicapped, or sibling groups. Couples seeking a healthy white infant sometimes turn to privately arranged adoptions where they are legal or will consider international adoption rather than accept one of the many children waiting for a family in this country.

Workers at the Children's Center are committed to placing as many children with families as possible and have considered expanding their services to single parents and nontraditional families. In addition, they are concerned that their follow-up counseling and infertility programs are not well utilized, because of emphasis on child placement issues. The director wonders if more active, effective programs such as these might enhance the adoption program by helping infertile couples become comfortable with adoption prospects and by providing counseling to maximize the success of the placements.

1. Is it appropriate to consider a marketing program for an agency that places children and deals with important issues?
2. What might be the goals of such a marketing effort?
3. How might the staff at the Children's Center apply the three parts of our marketing definition to their activities?
4. How would a well-focused marketing program help the Children's Center fulfill its mission?

5. If you were hired to build a marketing orientation for the Children's Center, what would be some of the elements of that approach?

FURTHER READING

Drucker, Peter F. What Business Can Learn from Nonprofits. *Harvard Business Review*, July–August 1989, 88–93.

Kotler, Philip. *Marketing for Nonprofit Organizations*. Englewood Cliffs, NJ: Prentice-Hall, 1982.

Kotler, Philip. *Principles of Marketing*. Englewood Cliffs, NJ: Prentice-Hall, 1986.

Lovelock, Christopher H. *Services Marketing*. Englewood Cliffs, NJ: Prentice-Hall, 1984.

Shapiro, Benson P. Marketing for Nonprofit Organizations. In *The Nonprofit Organization: Essential Readings*, edited by David L. Gies, J. Steven Ott, and Jay M. Shafritz, 262–270. Pacific Grove, CA: Brooks/Cole, 1990.

CHAPTER 2

Developing a Strategy: Strategic Planning and the Marketing Function

It is budget time at the Garden Center, and the board is trying to allocate its increasingly scarce resources. This proves, however, to be a difficult task. "Aren't we going to open our plant shop this year?" asked one board member. "No, I thought we were planning to focus on drawing more attendees to our spring flower show and not branch out into other businesses," replied another. This discussion continued for several hours, with a number of ideas for future programs and funding quickly suggested and rejected. As the meeting progressed, the board members became confused and frustrated and leaned toward refunding existing programs with a modest increment for inflation. After several hours, the committee was adjourned due to the pressing commitments of its members, and the issue of the budget was postponed until the next meeting.

This scenario is played out in the boardrooms of nonprofit organizations with appalling frequency. The leadership is trying to lead with no sense of direction, and the followers ultimately will have little choice but to travel the same convoluted path. Often dilemmas such as this are resolved at the final hour out of a sense of desperation. It is little wonder that organizations that lack direction have difficulty in getting anywhere at all.

Consider this. It's a lovely morning, and you get in your car. You put the keys in the ignition, pull out of the driveway, and get to the first intersection. "Hmm . . .," you say to yourself. "Turning right might be a splendid idea. Look at all the pretty green trees down there." At the next intersection, you are again faced with a decision. "I think I'll go straight here," you reason. "I turned right last time, and going straight will keep me going on a nice, steady course." After several hours of driving and decision making, you become somewhat weary of the process and wonder whether there was somewhere you ought to be going. Finally you conclude that you'd might as well head back home—back where you started from. "But wait a minute!" you think, "Where am I, and how do I get home from here?"

Most of us would scoff at this silly scenario and argue that we have far too much sense to undertake such a directionless journey. Yet it is not too farfetched an analogy to say that many of us act out this scenario daily in our work lives. Even large, multimillion dollar organizations often blunder ahead with little idea of where they would like to go or how to get there. It has been said that organizations that fail to plan should plan to fail. This catchy but somewhat oversimplified statement can tell us that the development of effective, well-thought-out plans are an ingredient of success.

Let's consider another hypothetical scenario: perhaps you have had the experience of being utterly lost and were relieved to find a phone booth to call the person you had set out to see and ask for directions. Unfortunately, the first question you will be asked is, "Well, where are you now?" If you haven't the foggiest idea, you are unlikely to receive much help. If a lack of clear direction and destination sounds like a difficult situation, consider this: many organizations don't even know where they are today!

STRATEGIC PLANNING AND ITS IMPORTANCE TO MARKETING

Although most organizations conduct some activities that they consider to be related to a broad definition of marketing, many never engage in any meaningful effort to define and determine the organization's overall goals and strategies. Marketing works to identify and satisfy wants and needs, and strategic planning works to identify organizational priorities. There is an important and essential partnership between the two activities.

An organization cannot successfully carry out a marketing program without making strategic decisions regarding its goals and priorities. The nonprofit first must have delineated desired outcomes, goals, and priorities in order to know how to market, what to market, to whom to market, and why the marketing task is important. Consider the following organizational priorities: reaching additional individual donors, bringing additional consumers to a new program, and recruiting and retaining high-quality employees to provide service. Each of these goals indicates the need for a very different marketing program, and the organization's marketing focus should support the achievement of these priorities.

Strategic planning cannot be meaningful without understanding the characteristics, wants, and needs of those to whom the organization wishes to market, attending to how they will be reached, and working to ensure their continued satisfaction. An organization that attempts to set goals and priorities for the future without focusing on the characteristics of the marketplace will find these goals to be limited and unrealistic. Marketing, then, plays a vital role in the setting of organizational strategy. The organization must consider the needs of vital groups, such as consumers, funders, and other stakeholders, if it is to map out a favorable direction.

The principles of strategic planning outlined in this chapter indicate an important set of considerations that go hand-in-hand with any marketing effort. The practitioner of nonprofit marketing must be sensitive to the fact that both the focus and tactics of marketing should be related closely to and supportive of the organization's overall strategic goals. The organization's marketing efforts will help it to achieve its goals in strategic positioning for the future. Marketing, when carried out effectively, is a highly strategic undertaking, clearly targeted to help the organization achieve a predefined, desired position in the marketplace. In short, organizational strategy must be geared to the market, and the marketing program must-be geared to this strategy if the nonprofit is to use its resources effectively and efficiently.

Strategic Planning as the Basis of the Marketing Effort

Any organization can choose to plan and take to market a wide range of offerings to a wide variety of potential consumers. There are decisions, then, to be made in determining what to offer, to whom, and how. Each organization differs in its choices; however, the decisions are made—whether deliberately or by default. These decisions form the basis of strategy.

An organization that offers well-targeted products and services that satisfy the consumer will improve its odds of success in fulfilling its mission and achieving financial stability. Strategic planning forms a framework for making organizational decisions in a way that makes sense, rather than in a haphazard manner that creates a poorly designed and unwieldy organization.

Sound strategic planning is vital to a well-planned marketing program. Marketing ideally should be an integrated part of the organization's operations and should support the organization's overall strategy. Without a clearly stated strategy, there could be a number of well-intentioned but fragmented marketing efforts supporting poorly conceived programs.

Let's look at an example of how strategic planning provides the basis of the marketing effort:

> A satellite health clinic has a mission of serving the needs of a low-income community. It finds that the community has a number of pressing needs, including the care of pregnant women, young children, and the elderly. From the standpoint of the marketing definition presented in chapter one, the clinic might effectively market to any one or all of these groups, identifying what is wanted and needed, bringing potential consumers to the clinic, and working toward their satisfaction.

The clinic, however, has limited human and financial resources. It is faced with decisions to make—which needs to serve and where to concentrate scarce resources. The clinic has several options. It can attempt to serve all three groups and face the possibility of doing poorly, or it can establish some priorities and plans that might include examining the urgency of the needs of each group, the organizational resources needed and available to serve those needs, and which other organizations might serve them.

The clinic needs to develop a strategy, to decide what it will and will not be. If it develops a strategic plan, this also might include a long-range vision of where the organization should be and how it might get there, year by year and step by step. Marketing to potential consumer groups without this framework for decision making could bankrupt the organization and compromise its ability to serve those clients it chooses to target.

If the clinic determines that there are alternate services available for pregnant women and children, it might decide to target the elderly as a priority group. This does not mean that the clinic will not continue to serve the others in some fashion or that it will not, in the future, plan to provide additional services. It indicates that the organization has determined a current strategy along with some long-range and strategic goals.

This example illustrates the fact that no organization has infinite resources and that developing plans and priorities is vital to effectively fulfilling its mission. Often, organizations lack a framework for making decisions and arbitrarily will blunder through a decision-making process without the facts. Strategic planning is a mechanism for information gathering, analysis, and exploration of alternatives that enables decisions of mission and allocation of resources to be made in a reasoned, relatively objective fashion.

Marketing is, then, an approach and a tool that assists the organization in reaching the goals it has decided upon and laid out in the strategic plan. After the "big picture" decisions have been made as a result of the planning process, the process of providing needed and wanted offerings, bringing consumers together with providers, and ensuring customer satisfaction can begin in earnest.

STRATEGIC, LONG-RANGE, AND SHORT-RANGE PLANNING

There are several different types of planning in an organization, and they are often the subject of some confusion. Let's clarify them:

- *Strategic planning* defines overall organizational goals and outlines a strategy for success. The strategic plan tells us where we're trying to go and specifies the ultimate destination.

- *Long-range planning* breaks down specific, operational plans over a multiyear time frame. It tells us what steps must be taken next year and the year after to achieve the goals we have set in our strategic plan.
- *Short-range planning* describes what we hope to accomplish this year. It tells us what moves we must make in the near future to achieve short-range goals and lay the groundwork for long-range and strategic plans.

As you might guess, planning is a process that builds on itself, and great interdependency is found among the three types of planning. The short-range plan should lay the foundation for the long-range plan by accomplishing appropriate goals. The long-range plan should specify actions and directions for reaching the goals set out in the strategic plan. It's like a pyramid, where the strategic plan forms a wide, solid base on which the organization stands. The long-range plan is the middle layer, which must be reached in order to accomplish strategic goals, and the short-range plan, although most immediate and visible, is only the tip of the iceberg, supported by a solid strategy for the future. It can be easy and tempting to form short-range plans first, but without a strategic direction these plans will stand alone and unsupported.

It is safe to say that most nonprofit organizations do not have a clear strategic plan. Even those who say they do rarely write out the specifics of what the organization should do, accomplish, and become in the next several years. Most organizations have short-range plans that often are in the form of annual goals and objectives, a budget, or plans to deal with specific situations or events. However, these plans typically lack a substantial basis on which day-to-day decisions can rest.

It is an interesting exercise to ask top management and board members, without warning, to write down their vision of what the organization hopes to accomplish and what the organization should be within five years. Some simply may have no idea, and others will outline a grand vision that is, unfortunately, shared by no one. The sad fact is that even the people who lead the organization sometimes have no sense of direction and often lead in the manner described at the beginning of this chapter—by deciding to turn right here and left there because it seems, at the time, to be the thing to do.

WHY STRATEGIC PLANNING?

Many organizations fail to see the importance of having a sound strategic plan, preferring to live from day to day and trusting their instincts to carry them into the future. However, the world in which we live is rapidly changing, and an effective organization needs to identify and creatively respond to these changes. Strategic planning can help an organization prepare for the future in some important ways:

- Identification of trends in the external environment that will impact the way it does business
- Examination of the organization's history and current capabilities
- Delineation of strategic alternatives
- Analysis of the pros and cons of those alternatives
- Choosing a specific, well-defined strategy
- Operationalizing plans into concrete, measurable action steps

Although the planning process does not guarantee a spectacular outcome or an added measure of success, it is a useful tool in providing a framework and a set of common goals for the organization's operations. It helps an organization to make the decisions it must make in any case.

RESISTANCE TO STRATEGIC PLANNING

Most nonprofits do not have well-defined strategic plans that guide them into the future. The reasons for this are varied, but they may include these classic statements:

- **"We don't have the time for all that."** Many administrators believe that their staffs are working at capacity and could not possibly take on any additional responsibility. Granted, significant time and energy are involved in the planning effort, but without it the organization is adrift, spending time in a haphazard manner.

- **"Things change too fast—there's no point in trying to plan."** Effective strategic planning helps in tracking and staying on top of the rapid change many organizations face. An important component of any planning effort is identifying trends in the external environment and developing strategies to respond to them.

- **"It seems to be a waste of time to go through a strategic planning effort when new situations always come up—we don't want to be tied to a predetermined plan if opportunity knocks."** There is no such thing as a perfect strategic plan; to develop one would require a clear vision of the future that we mortals lack. No plan should preclude management decision making and remove discretion over whether to implement or change the plan. In fact, a useful outcome of the planning process is the development of a process for evaluating ideas and monitoring the organization's progress and options.

- **"Planning is too academic and esoteric and only produces attrac-**

tive documents to sit on a shelf. While we're busy sitting around planning, everybody else will pass us by." Like any management function, planning can be done well or badly. Planning has, and sometimes deserves, a bad reputation for producing endless charts, graphs, verbiage, and little action. If this is all that is produced in the planning process, it is indeed a futile exercise. The production of useless plans is a reflection of useless planning; in contrast, effective planning is a proactive, dynamic, ongoing process that provides effective plans.

• "The administration (and/or board) always shoots from the hip anyway—there's no reason to develop plans no one will follow." An organization that finds itself in this predicament does face a problem in its strategic planning efforts. It is always difficult and sometimes impossible to develop and implement plans without the support of those in power. They might be wooed and drawn into the process at some point, but to be effective, planning must be supported from the top down.

The bottom line is that strategic planning at its best provides management with a thorough, reasoned, objective look at the past, the present, and future scenarios. However, like any management tool, planning can be misused—for supporting decisions that have already been made, for furthering the favored projects of a few in power, or for developing an attractive document for presentation at ceremonial occasions.

Above all, planning must be a well-organized effort. The idea of planning for the future is new to many, and staff and board members will need to be educated and involved in the process if it is to be successful. Many well-intentioned organizations have formed planning committees only to have their activities put on the back burner or stalled due to a lack of direction and leadership. Developing a plan for planning may sound like a compulsive person's dream, but knowing how the plan is to be developed will avoid false starts and confusion. Using a process such as the one outlined in this chapter will give an organization a starting point from which to tailor a process that responds to its unique capabilities, issues, and needs.

WHO IS A NONPROFIT PLANNER?

Organizations vary in the degree to which they embrace the principles of participative management, allowing decision making to be a group process. However, effective planning involves a wide representation of those affected by the plans and those responsible for their implementation.

One way to involve staff and board members in the process is to form a planning committee. Committees, in some circles, have a bad name, carrying such designations as "a group that takes minutes and wastes hours" and "a group that individually can do nothing but collectively decides that nothing can be done." Sadly, in some cases such a reputation is deserved; however, there also are effective, exciting committees that accomplish the task at hand, as well as build a committed team. Strategic planning committees are vital to the work of the organization. It simply is not possible for the organization to plan without the input, involvement, and blessing of a variety of individuals, including the board, top and middle management, and the staff who is out in the trenches on a daily basis.

How and by whom strategic planning is done is of vital importance. In fact, wise planners sometimes will sacrifice technical excellence for human acceptance. Planning is, above all, a process that can provide for opportunities in team building and the development of creative approaches to problem solving. At times, a plan can be effective even when it seems to state the obvious because it has successfully rallied the organization around the commonsense approach.

In some organizations, strategic planning is board driven, with members of the staff serving as support or resource persons. In others, management staff members pull together the plan, and the board approves it after a brief review. In fact, neither of these approaches represents the ideal. Probably the best approach to strategic planning is a partnership between board and management, with input from all levels of the staff. Ideally, the strategic plan represents the collective vision of those responsible for the organization's future success and creates a future acceptable to all.

In small organizations, everyone can be a planner. Although members of the janitorial staff and typing pool might not be expected to take the lead in planning efforts, the future direction of the organization has an impact on them, and they should be involved and informed. Even in large organizations, information can be shared with staff at all levels and their input solicited through their supervisors or group information meetings. Staff members who are involved in day-to-day operations can have refreshing insights into organizational issues—this can be important especially in large organizations where top management may be far removed from those who serve on the "front lines." In any case, when involvement in planning is spread among board and staff, the plan is more likely to receive widespread acceptance and implementation.

In many nonprofit organizations, there are several committed constituencies that should be considered in the planning process. One of the characteristics of the effective nonprofit organization is its commitment to mission and to those it exists to serve. Volunteers, clients, and many other groups in the community may have psychological ownership of the organization, and in many cases, this ownership should translate into involvement in the strategic planning process. Although the different perspectives of varied constituents can enrich the organization and bring new ideas, they also can prove to be a complicating factor. People often associate with nonprofit organizations because their interests are satisfied by this affiliation. This commitment can restrict the organization's options because each of the important groups can bring an additional herd of sacred cows to the planning effort. Plans that increase efficiency or profitability, seemingly noble goals, may prove unacceptable if they are perceived as interfering with the unique characteristics of the nonprofit that motivated the involvement and support of important groups.

INGREDIENTS OF THE PLANNING PROCESS

Although strategic planning is a management tool that can be carried out in a variety of ways, there basically are three phases to the strategic planning process:

A. Analysis and synthesis
    1. Identification of current strategy
    2. Internal analysis
    3. External analysis
    4. SWOT analysis (strengths, weaknesses, opportunities, threats)
B. Strategy development
    1. Development of an organizational mission
    2. Identification of strategic alternatives
    3. Determination of long- and short-term strategies
    4. Setting of goals and objectives
    5. Development of action plans
C. Implementation and revision
    1. Monitoring of plan implementation
    2. Update/revision of plans

Each of these phases represents unique functions and tasks and is designed to assist the organization in examining its past, present, and possible future scenarios. We'll discuss each of these phases and what typically is accomplished in some detail.

Analysis and Synthesis

Prior to setting goals and formulating organizational strategies, the organization will need to gather information regarding itself and the environment in which it operates. This step may be a major or minor one in terms of the time and resources it consumes, depending largely on whether the organization routinely gathers and analyzes such data.

In any case, this phase of planning will allow the organization to develop solid groundwork on which to develop and justify its eventual strategies.

Identification of Current Strategy.   As we illustrated above, an important part of a successful journey is knowing where you are starting from. This might be thought of as the identification of current strategy. It always is a useful exercise to determine what the organization's strategy has been and how the organization has fared. Even if there never has been a discussion of strategy, every organization has one by default. These statements might represent the strategies of some hapless organizations:

- We chase funding and provide any type of programming for which money is easily available at the moment.
- This organization follows the lead of several wealthy and influential board members, who have pet interests and call all the shots.
- Our strategy is to attempt to serve our clients without going broke; we try to provide whatever they need and don't worry much about where the money will come from.

Although it is highly unlikely that these "statements of strategy" would be found in any organization's publicity packet, they reflect the de facto strategies of many organizations. Organizations also might have well-developed strategies, which are the organization's starting point.

Determining the organization's present strategy might be a simple task if it has been clearly stated and, for the most part, followed; however, in many cases the strategy is not overt or easily identified. Looking at program records can determine the facts regarding the program's past, and knowledgeable staff and/or board members might assist in developing a profile of the past strategy.

Internal Analysis.   A thorough internal analysis will be essential to the organization's ultimate ability to assess itself; its capabilities, history, successes, and failures all are important to the organization's ability to plan for the future. An honest, complete diagnostic check on the organization will form the basis for strategy down the line. Also, the nonprofit must pay attention to internal stakeholders, such as the staff, board, volunteers, and consumers. No strategy, however brilliant, will succeed without the support of important internal groups such as these. In order to determine strategy, the organization must look at what it can do and what it has done in the past. This is the role of the internal analysis.

External Analysis. There are many forces in the external environment that affect the way the organization must do business. There is no doubt that a variety of social, economic, and political trends have changed the mission, the offerings, and the day-to-day functioning of many nonprofits. The organization, then, must identify and track these trends in order to be more responsive to the needs it exists to serve and to develop sound strategies for the future.

An organization must know whether funding cuts are in the wind, whether the demographics of its service area are changing, and whether it is feasible to meet the needs of different, sophisticated consumers. Otherwise, it will have significant difficulties in becoming, and maintaining, a viable presence in a competitive marketplace.

SWOT Analysis. The SWOT analysis is a way of taking inventory of the organization's present situation and potential future options. It involves the identification of the strengths, weaknesses, opportunities, and threats faced by an organization. These form the basis of the strategic plan.

Strengths generally are regarded as internal aspects of the situation, in that they reflect the things the organization does well and can build upon. Strengths can include a highly skilled staff, financial solvency, a good reputation, and the availability of attractive physical space. Strengths also suggest directions the organization can take in the future:

- A skilled staff has the capability to develop new programs or take on additional responsibilities.
- A financially sound organization is able to undertake new programs that involve some risk or expand existing offerings.
- A positive reputation forms the basis of expansion into related areas; clients and referrals are gained more easily.
- Available space allows the organization to expand programs and serve additional needs without the burden of seeking an expansion site.

Weaknesses also are internal to the organization; they are the organization's shortcomings, although they are not always anyone's fault. They can include problems inherent in the field or situations that have arisen unexpectedly.

Weaknesses also can be important in identifying strategies that will or will not be effective for the organization:

- A shortage of funding necessitates reordering priorities or placing more emphasis on seeking alternative funds.

- A program with a poor reputation is the target for extinction, revamping, or a good PR job.
- The organization that is unable to attract and retain qualified professionals needs to develop new strategies as part of its plan for future success.

Opportunities often are the foundation of organizational strategies and generally reflect situations external to the organization. Although some organizations are opportunistic by nature, rarely do organizations systematically identify the variety of potential opportunities they face. There are many facets to an organization, and especially in larger organizations, the awareness of opportunities is compartmental and discipline-specific, so that the finance department identifies financial opportunities and program personnel know programmatic expansion potential. Identification of the alternatives for the organization can point the way to lucrative, expedient strategies. These opportunities form the basis of future success:

- Grant money that is available for certain programs provides an opportunity for expansion without excessive risk.
- A weak competitor allows the organization easy entry into an area where unsatisfied, unserved consumers have few allegiances.
- A potential partner shares resources, allows programmatic expansion, and capitalizes on the strengths of both organizations.

Threats are factors external to the organization that must be considered when developing strategies. Nearly all organizations face an environment that is loaded with pitfalls and roadblocks to success. These threats may be specific to an individual program, the organization, the field, or nonprofit organizations as a whole. The identification of organizational threats provides the basis for strategy development to avoid adverse consequences of the threats or at least work around them. Threats can take many forms and can include:

- Legislation that cuts deductions and therefore, incentives for charitable giving
- A competing organization that is targeting the same type of consumer, donor, referral agent, or funding
- New regulations that make operations more difficult and costly
- A shortage of trained personnel who are vital to service delivery

Some organizations conduct a SWOT analysis and don't know what to do with it; it looks good, feels official, but does not seem applicable to reality. The ideal situation, of course, is to turn weaknesses into strengths and threats into opportunities. This is not always feasible, but it is possible to step back after completing the SWOT analysis and try to determine what actions are suggested by this exercise. This then becomes fodder for the next step in the planning process.

Strategy Development

After the organization has completed the work outlined above, it is ready to look at that information and its implications for the future. Internal, external, and SWOT analyses have identified some options and potential courses of action; the next step is to add to and choose among those options.

Development of an Organizational Mission.   Most organizations have a mission statement. There is, however, an excellent chance that it is in need of revision and updating as part of the strategic planning process. Although some insist that mission development should be the initial step in strategic planning, this vital exercise should not take place in a vacuum. The data gathering conducted in the first phase of the planning process is essential to consideration of the mission; examining what the organization has been doing and what is happening in the external environment will provide clues as to what direction the mission will need to take in the future to ensure that the organization remains vital and responsive to actual needs.

The mission statement is an important document that should outline the organization's strategic direction and clearly state its business. The mission statement should, at a minimum, tell:

1. What the organization is and does
2. Why it exists
3. Who it serves

Let's look at one organization's mission statement:

> NewLife Rehabilitation Center serves adults and adolescents on whose lives drug and alcohol abuse have had a negative impact. NewLife provides assessment, outpatient counseling, and residential rehabilitation services to drug and alcohol abusers, their families, and significant others using the basic principles of Alcoholics and Narcotics Anonymous.

This statement tells the reader what the organization does and why it exists, along with a brief description of the type of clientele it seeks to serve. The statement is broad enough to allow for new services without revamping the mission statement. For example, NewLife might add recreation programs for addicted teens or support groups for the spouses of cocaine abusers without violating the mission. Suppose, however, the Center studied the changing demographics of drug abuse and decided to add programs for addicted infants or elementary school-aged drug abusers. This would call for a significant change in the direction of the organization, and therefore, updating the mission statement.

A mission statement can become obsolete quickly as the organization adapts to a changing environment or may be in need of revision because of flaws in its initial composition. A mission statement can miss the mark in a number of ways:

- It is so broad that it does not describe sufficiently why the organization exists or differentiate it from others.
- It is so narrow that it does not allow the organization room for growth and development; it will soon be outdated.
- It is long and rambling, talking in detail about what programs and services are offered and why. The reader must sift through many words in an effort to determine the meaning.
- It details the organization's original mission, which may have changed significantly so that the statement is no longer relevant.

Review of the mission statement is an exercise that can begin early in the planning process, but reasonably cannot conclude until the setting of strategic vision is complete. If the organization decides to pursue a bold new direction or scrap the existing strategy, this will impact its statement of mission.

In deciding on the organization's mission, there are several fundamental questions that should be considered:

- What business are we in?
- What will happen if we stay in that business?
- What business do we want to be in?

The answer to the first question should be obvious after an initial review and, if needed, after an update of the mission statement. The statement should reflect the organization's current interests and activities, and an organization that has difficulty pinpointing what business it currently is in will have to tackle a major task prior to proceeding with the planning process. The next two steps, however, are considerably trickier.

Many businesses, nonprofit and for-profit, have found that they need to make substantial changes in the definition of their business and how it is carried out. Thus, telephone companies have become communication businesses; steel companies have developed into multi-business conglomerates; and department stores have diversified to include beauty salons, insurance companies, and real estate firms. Many nonprofits have found that their missions have broadened to allow for some inescapable realities as well, such as the need for child and adult daycare for two-income or single-parent families, AIDS services, and programs for the homeless.

In some cases, organizations that fail to change their missions face extinction. Programs for the elderly once were geared toward the support of frail old persons waiting to die—they now include aerobics classes, travel programs, and opportunities for romance among an increasingly larger and healthier senior population. Similarly, organizations now exist to support and counsel stepfamilies, and others provide programs for new mothers over thirty or even forty. All of these offerings might have been unnecessary and poorly utilized in the recent past, but may be booming businesses today. Continual adjustment of the organization's mission and line of business will keep it vital and interesting in a changing environment.

The internal and external analyses also will give the planners of the organization's future a good idea of the business it should be in. In some cases, the organization may be approaching obsolescence, and an examination of the current needs of the community served will help to determine what business direction the organization should be in to meet current and future needs.

Identification of Strategic Alternatives.   The analysis and synthesis that forms the initial part of the planning process should identify a number of potential strategies for the organization. These might come from the external, internal, and SWOT analyses. The planning process also should encourage the exploration of ideas that may have been "bouncing around" in the organization for some time.

This step in the planning process lends itself to a brainstorming or creative-thinking approach, as those involved in the planning process can share even the most farfetched ideas without fear of ridicule. However, as in any business undertaking, ideas must be supported with substance, and it is the task of the planners to be certain that each alternative is rational and feasible. Supporting data gathered in the initial phase of planning can be useful here, or additional data gathering might be needed.

Many organizations have found that the development of board/staff planning committees or task forces have been effective in accomplishing the work involved in the planning process, without overburdening a few individuals. This approach allows for the exploration of several alternatives or issues simultaneously, with each group issuing a recommendation on the area it has studied to a central planning committee composed of key board and staff members. In this way, involvement in the planning process is maximized, and alternatives can be evaluated painlessly prior to proceeding further in strategy development.

The essence of strategic planning, then, is the ability to identify and prioritize strategic alternatives, fitting them into the organization's mission and the needs of those it exists to serve. In the case of a domestic violence center, for example, the decision makers might face a number of issues:

- Should this organization attempt to address all of the needs of victims of abuse?
- Should it focus on adults and children equally?
- Should it gear services toward support during a crisis or commit itself to the often long-term task of rebuilding lives?
- To what extent should the agency serve as an information and referral service rather than a direct provider?
- Should it offer services to adult male as well as female victims?
- Should it offer services to abusers as well as the abused?

Table 2-1 might represent a few of the specific strategic alternatives and their rationales developed by a planning committee for the domestic violence agency.

These represent only a few of the alternatives the agency might face in the future; all may be legitimate needs, but resources may be lacking to pursue each program simultaneously. Therefore, the planning process should include a detailed study of these programs, with an outcome of set priorities and allocation of resources that ideally will serve the clients and provide a good fit with the organization's capabilities. The organization can explore a variety of possibilities, including networking with other organizations that provide educational, legal, and economic assistance to avoid duplicating services.

Obviously, there is no absolute technology associated with the planning process, which in the final analysis is more an art than a science. The relationship to the marketing function, however, is clear: the organization's planning efforts must identify the wants and needs of clients, determine how its offerings can be brought to potential consumers, and work to assure that it will satisfy those consumers.

Setting of Goals and Objectives.   An important part of determining and working toward organizational priorities is the setting of goals and

TABLE 2-1   Strategic Alternatives and Their Rationales

Alternative	Rationale
Develop additional information and counseling related to education and training	Internal analysis shows that many clients will need additional training to become self-supporting
Provide counseling, support, and recreational groups for children ages 5–12	Few resources for preadolescent children with histories of abuse and unstable families are available in this area
Increase the availability of free or low-cost legal assistance to clients	Internal and external data show that domestic violence is increasing in the area and that victims often lack financial resources to pay for services
Facilitate the availability of short-term economic assistance to middle-income families in transition	Program records and national data show that many women seeking independence initially are unable to support their families and need help while a divorce settlement and job training are in process

objectives. This process makes concrete and operative the good ideas the organization has developed and helps build mechanisms by which these ideas can be implemented, then monitored.

A goal is a statement that describes an intent or desired outcome in broad terms. It tells what the organization is trying to accomplish. Goals should reflect the organization's overall planning process and should clearly outline organizational priorities. Examples:

- Within the next five years, KidCare will reach full utilization in its existing daycare center and will expand into two additional communities.
- The Neighborhood Community Center will work to serve additional needs next fiscal year by expanding its weekend programming for teenagers.
- The City Children's Museum will increase its net revenues by 10 percent within the next three years.
- Ourtown Home Health Agency will double the number of clients it serves within five years.

In each of these cases, the goal states what the organization is attempting to do, but does not indicate how it will be accomplished. The how is explained by outlining an objective or series of objectives. Objectives tell what the organization specifically proposes to do in order to reach the goals set. The following might be a few appropriate objectives for the KidCare daycare center, which seeks to increase utilization and expand into additional sites:

- Increase advertising and promotional budgets by 5 percent per year
- Work with local corporations to promote services and attempt to arrange contracts
- Initiate quarterly satisfaction surveys aimed at retention of clients
- Conduct demographic studies of area communities to determine likely sites for expansion

In this way, the organization becomes more specific by mapping out tactics that will help it to reach its strategic goals. Without this level of specificity, it is easy to determine and state grand goals and objectives that are impractical or unachievable. The delineation of clear, measurable objectives forces the planners to develop a clear pathway to the desired destination and provides a direction to follow and monitor.

Setting short-term strategies and priorities is a relatively easy undertaking; most managers are accustomed to taking charge and deciding what will be accomplished within the next week, month, or year. The setting of long-term goals is more difficult and in many ways, more important, for example:

> An organization that has a vision of developing a major regional arts festival must work toward that goal gradually from humble beginnings and must court artists, supporters, funders, and individuals influential in the local and regional arts to accomplish this goal. This organization, then, would have a clear long-term strategy, supported by a number of short-term strategies.
>
> **Long-term goal:**
> To build a major regional arts festival
> **Short-term goals:**
> To initiate a small local arts festival
> To attract an increasing number of artists to participate
> To increase funding each year and allow for expansion
> To boost attendance at the festival each year
> To expand the advertising and public relations efforts
> To attract attendees from a wider geographic area each year

As this example shows, a single long-term strategic goal must be supported by a number of short-range and long-range goals if it is to be accomplished. The organization must determine its ultimate destination and then outline a multiyear course of action that systematically will build toward that goal. Ideally, each of these goals will be accompanied by one or more objectives that will outline the mechanisms for achieving those goals.

Development of Action Plans.   The next and final level of the strategic planning process typically is the development of action plans. Action plans specify exactly what is to be done, when, and by whom. It is at this level that the nuts and bolts of planning are carried out to support the grand schemes and strategies that have been developed. In large corporations, action plans might be developed by the lower levels of management who hold responsibility for carrying out the day-to-day work of the organization.

In any case, it is important to be specific about what actions are needed to support the organization's plans. Action plans can include several items, such as:

- Action step—tells exactly what is to be done, including hiring staff, beginning a new project, acquiring a facility, or ordering office equipment for a new venture.
- Person responsible—indicates, by position or name, who will take responsibility for the completion of the action.
- Initiation and completion dates—specify when the activity is to be started and a target date for completion of the project.

Although some managers resist this level of detail, it is important for the organization to be specific and to provide enough information so that the plans can be implemented even if key people leave the organization or if, down the line, the staff members fail to remember a commitment made several years ago.

Implementation and Revision

Efforts at organizational planning most often fail at two stages: the beginning and the end. Organizations may become bogged down in detail and day-to-day operations and fail to get the project started, or they may develop a plan and allow it to gather dust, reverting to crisis management. The latter is the more tragic, as it represents a waste of staff time and energy and can be demoralizing to those whose good ideas and careful plans are ignored. Implementation, then, is when plans become reality.

Monitoring of Plan Implementation.   Management consultant Peter Drucker stated, "Sooner or later, even good ideas must degenerate into work." Implementation of a strategic plan is the point at which the lofty, visionary work of planning comes to rolling up one's sleeves and placing emphasis on action.

Many organizations disband or dismantle planning groups when the initial work is done, ignoring that in many ways the most important part is to follow. It is of vital importance that the planning effort be ongoing, in recognition of the fact that planning is a process, not an event. The development of detailed action plans will provide a natural and easily followed framework for implementation and monitoring; the planning group will need only to pull out well-documented plans and discuss whether the action plans have been implemented and what the results have been. This discussion should be geared toward determining progress or lack thereof, clearly communicating accountability and responsibility.

Plans are less likely to become attractive shelf ornaments if those involved know that they will be called upon to discuss their role in implementation; the "public humiliation factor" can be very powerful: knowing that a loss in esteem, merit, and possibly employment can result from a failure to work with the plan. Meetings should be held at least quarterly to monitor and discuss progress towards goals and objectives set during the planning process.

Update/Revision of Plans.   It should be painfully obvious to all those attempting to plan for the organization's future that both internal and external circumstances are changing continually. Developing and rigidly adhering to plans is by no means the goal; as a matter of fact, it is a mark of poor management. There continually is a need to update and revise plans that may have been ideal at the time they were developed, but will not stay in tune with a changing reality.

Any effective organization allows for the revision of plans taking into account both changes in the operating realities it faces and new ideas and developments. Again, this supports the need for an ongoing planning and evaluation effort. The planning approach described in this chapter should become a part of standard operating procedure, with all decisions examined from the standpoints of strategy and their viability in the marketplace. Therefore, at least quarterly, new information that might impact the update or revision of plans should become a part of that organization's agenda.

CONCLUSION

It is important for the nonprofit organization to realize that marketing is not a process that will spring magically from the collective inspiration of its leadership. Rather, the marketing process begins with the development of organizational strategy, and the strategy development process must include consideration of marketing principles.

The organization that uses the process outlined in this chapter to develop organizational strategy will find that its marketing plan and marketing strategies will flow readily out of the strategic plan. An organization that ignores the need for an overall strategy can easily find that it is wasting marketing resources by chasing programs or activities that are not strategic priorities within the organization.

REVIEW QUESTIONS

1. What is meant by strategic planning, long-range planning, and short-range planning? How would you respond to someone who claimed that strategic and long-range planning are synonymous?

2. What are some of the major organizational benefits in having a strategic plan?

3. Why do managers tend to resist strategic planning? How might you counter some of their objections?

4. Why is strategic planning important to the marketing effort?

5. Does an organization that lacks a strategic plan necessarily lack a strategy? What is the relationship between the two?

6. How does a SWOT analysis assist an organization in strategy formulation?

7. What are some of the characteristics of an effective mission statement?

8. How does an organization best identify and prioritize strategic alternatives?

9. What is meant by goals and objectives? Why are they important in the planning process?

10. What are some of the key factors in monitoring plan implementation? In updating and revising plans?

MINI CASE STUDY

Jobs for People is a private, nonprofit organization that has existed for ten years and is contemplating its future. Its mission statement is as follows:

> Jobs for People provides counseling, training, and support for unemployed, underemployed, or dissatisfied workers. The organization's goal is to assist the individual in exploring his/her unique skills, abilities, aptitudes, and preferences in order to achieve optimal job satisfac-

tion. Jobs for People does not provide job placement but works with clients to help them to reach the resources they need to find, keep, and enjoy their life's work.

Jobs for People started out in an economically distressed area that had been hard-hit with layoffs and cutbacks by local manufacturers. When this organization began operation, it was flooded with unemployed skilled and semiskilled laborers who needed assistance in reassessing how to support their families. Originally, Jobs for People hung posters in unemployment and food stamp offices and informed the social workers in the agencies that dealt with the unemployed of their services.

Ten years later, the picture has changed in the communities served by Jobs for People. Many of those victims of the cutbacks by local manufacturers have retired, relocated, or retrained, and the area's unemployment rate is low. However, many of the positions now available are in the relatively low-paying service sector, creating a different type of economic and employment problem.

Now Jobs for People's clients are different, plus many of the original clients are returning and expressing dissatisfaction with what they see as limited options in the jobs to which they retreated. The organization also is seeing more women who are reentering the work force after taking off several years to raise children, and it is discovering a growing number of clients who are college educated but feel dissatisfied and directionless.

The organization's old ways of marketing have become ineffective, and the board and management are aware that the clients and perhaps even the mission of the organization have changed. They are beginning to wonder what direction to take in offering and marketing new services, and whether some entirely new direction might be needed.

1. What are some of the major strategic issues facing Jobs for People at present?
2. What would be the benefits of strategic planning for this organization? What might happen if the organization fails to plan for the future?
3. How would you use the three major phases of the strategic planning process outlined in this chapter to guide the organization to a better future? What are some of the major factors that would need to be addressed at each point?

FURTHER READING

Alexander, John O. Planning and Management in Nonprofit Organizations. In *The Nonprofit Organization: Essential Readings*, edited by David L. Gies, J. Steven Ott, and Jay M. Shafritz, 155–166. Pacific Grove, CA: Brooks/Cole, 1990.

Barry, Bryan W. *Strategic Planning Workbook for Nonprofit Organizations*. St. Paul, MN: Amherst H. Wilder Foundation, 1986.

Espy, Siri N. *Handbook of Strategic Planning for Nonprofit Organizations*. New York: Praeger Publishers, 1986.

————. Planning for Success: Strategic Planning in Nonprofits. *Nonprofit World*, 6(5): September/October 1988, 23–24.

————. Putting Your Plan into Action. *Nonprofit World*, 7(1): January/February 1989, 27–28.

————. Where Are You, and Where Do You Think You're Going? *Nonprofit World*, 6(6): November/December 1988, 19–20.

Flexner, William A., Eric Berkowitz, and Montague Brown. (eds.). *Strategic Planning in Health Care Management*. Rockville, MD: Aspen Systems Corporation, 1981.

Twining, Fred N., Ph.D., Robert A. Derzon, and Charles S. McCoy, Ph.D. Managing Values Through Planning. *Health Management Quarterly*, 9(4): Fourth Quarter 1987, 15–17.

CHAPTER 3

Knowing Your Customer

Sarah is a young, recently divorced mother, struggling to cope with two unruly toddlers and a messy, run-down apartment. She knows she should look for work, but since her mother died, she has no one to watch the kids. Also, she really can't afford a sitter. She wonders how she can continue to deal with these overwhelming problems. Sarah realizes that she is becoming depressed and needs someone to talk to. One of her neighbors had told her about the counseling center across town, but Sarah was reluctant to call. "The center is in a fancy part of town," she muses, "and it would take two buses to get there. Besides, I'd be embarrassed to tell them I can't afford to pay."

Nonprofit consumers come in all shapes and sizes. Young and old, rich and poor, seeking enrichment and survival, nonprofit organizations serve them all. Some organizations, such as a zoo or a hospital, may exist to serve a wide spectrum of the population. Others may be narrowly focused on serving the needs of emotionally disturbed adolescent males or the sufferers of a rare disease. In any case, an organization that is in business to serve cannot do so without looking at the needs of its constituents and attempting to meet them.

Profit-oriented businesses know that understanding and appealing to the consumer is good business. A field trip to the grocery store should provide ample proof. The sugary cereals are placed on the bottom shelves, easily reachable for the young customer who can sing the jingles before learning the ABCs. There are pink and blue diapers decorated with cartoon characters for wearers who will worry little about their aesthetics when putting them to their unglamorous use. Dog food comes dyed and shaped like chops, even though its ultimate consumers are colorblind and unappreciative of this artistry. However, these seemingly shameless gimmicks sell products because they reflect an awareness of the consumer market. Their manufacturers understand that there are many factors in moving the product off the shelves. Look at the lessons that nonprofit organizations can learn from for-profit businesses:

- The person who controls the purse strings may not be the ultimate consumer, so marketing must be aimed at those who make the purchasing decision as well as those who consume.

- Those making decisions that affect the organization will have a number of influences, including advertising, word-of-mouth, and the opinions and desires of significant others.

- Strict utility value is not enough—consumers and other important groups are looking for products that serve basic needs with a flair or an extra appeal.

- The product or service should be placed where it is easily accessible by those who will make recommendations or decisions regarding utilization, donations, and other desired outcomes.

- Never underestimate the power of human emotions—the desire to serve and satisfy loved ones is strong and often will triumph over reason.

Not surprisingly, consumer psychology also must be learned by the nonprofit organization seeking to make an impact. Unfortunately, nonprofits sometimes fail to understand the complexity of the marketplace in which they must succeed. The marketing task often is a very difficult one, with many different groups to reach in many different ways.

RESOURCE ATTRACTION AND ALLOCATION

In the case of consumer products and services, it is hoped that sales of the product will generate enough funds to manufacture more products or to offer additional services, which will then be sold and produce more cash. This cycle represents the expected performance of American business in its simplest form; the more the product or service is utilized, the more money is produced, and the more profit is generated. The consumer is expected to reimburse the producer for the cost of the product as well as provide a profit to compensate the investors or owners of the business for the use of their capital. This system, when it works, provides the consumer with needed and wanted offerings and the business with an adequate return on its investment, and everyone is happy. If the product does not produce the desired financial return, it likely will be a target for extinction.

In many nonprofit settings, however, the process is not so simple. Think of the work of a food bank. Having a large base of consumers will not enrich the organization; in fact, the more people who utilize the service, the faster its resources will be depleted. By definition, consumers cannot be expected to provide reimbursement for the services they use. However, in terms of mission fulfillment, the more the resources of the organization are consumed, the more successful the organization is in fulfilling its mission of feeding the hungry. This organization does not follow a cycle in which its services produce cash for use in providing additional services. In this case, there is a straight line flow of resources—directly out of the organization. Resources, then, must be replenished through a separate process if the organization is to survive.

The nonprofit organization typically has two major financial tasks:

- **Resource attraction** is the process through which the nonprofit organization brings funds, volunteers, board members, and other necessary ingredients into the organization to enable it to do business. Resources can come from a variety of sources, including fees for service, donations from individuals, corporations, and foundations, or funding from government agencies. These resources are not always financial in nature and can include volunteerism or donations of goods and services.

- **Resource allocation** is the process of using or expending the financial resources in an effective, efficient manner in order to fulfill the organization's mission. The organization must allocate resources among its personnel, material and capital needs, and often among different programs and services within the organization. Typically, this is done through a budgeting process during which financial decisions are made that will affect the organization's ability to deliver services.

Both resource attraction and resource allocation are related to the organization's marketing efforts. Resource attraction requires an organized marketing approach, and resource allocation decisions should be the result of a strategic planning process that provides the organization with an understanding of the priority needs and wants it will serve to fulfill its mission.

THE IMPORTANCE OF RESOURCE ATTRACTION AS A MARKETING TASK

Often, the nonprofit organization must market both to those who will fund and to those who will use their services. Resource attraction almost always is a marketing consideration for the nonprofit, although the emphasis will depend upon a number of factors, including the financial position of the program or organization. However, even organizations that do not have immediate "need" place an emphasis on attracting funds; a major nonprofit with a large endowment may place more emphasis on attracting new resources than would a grassroots organization that is struggling to survive.

Nonprofit programs usually can be categorized according to their financial "neediness" within the organization, which some might see as a rough measure of the urgency of resource attraction:

1. Resource consuming programs. Some programs consume resources without directly generating a financial return. Food banks, shelters for the homeless, and emergency relief services are examples of programs that are not reimbursed directly. Recipients are not expected to be capable of paying for services, and in many cases, the organization has more "customers" than it can serve. In situations such as this,

the program depends wholly on resource attraction. Marketing the program to potential funders is the primary marketing task.

2. Partially self-supporting programs. Some programs generate funding from products or services that is inadequate to support their existence. Examples can include mental health services offered on a sliding scale according to income and admission fees to a museum or an event that defray but do not cover total costs. In this case, marketing to funders and consumers equally is important, and organizations even attempt to attract "paying customers" in order to provide funds to subsidize the services provided to those who cannot pay.

3. Breakeven programs. Some programs generate enough funds to cover all costs but do not produce a surplus. This can result from a fluke in the marketplace or can be by design, in which the organization is reimbursed by a funder on a cost basis or chooses to offer the program or service strictly at cost for mission-related reasons. In the long-run, programs that operate without surplus funds are in a precarious position, since there is no cushion for difficult times or funding for new programs that will need subsidy during startup. In this case, the organization concentrates on attracting the consumers who provide the cash to fund day-to-day operations, but reaching donors is important to provide a needed surplus.

4. Profitable programs. Some programs generate an actual excess of revenue over expense. These can include a nursing home or a daycare center directed at middle- and upper-income consumers. Although many nonprofits dream of the luxury of having profitable programs, they are faced with a dual marketing task of ensuring utilization by appropriate consumers and raising funds. Even if resource attraction is not a necessity for survival, donated funds can provide additional means for expanding programs or allowing the subsidy of other programs and services.

TO WHOM DOES THE NONPROFIT MARKET?

Nonprofit organizations face a very complex marketplace. Not only are funding and consuming separate issues, but there are a number of separate groups that the organization must consider in its efforts to effectively market services.

Although the for-profit business has stockholders who benefit financially from the success of the organization, the nonprofit has a number of individuals and groups who have a stake in its continued existence on a practical or emotional level. In fact, all the groups mentioned can be defined as stakeholders, because they are affected by the work of the organization and suffer a negative impact should it face extinction.

Stakeholders in any category also might be tapped as sources of funding, referrals, board membership, employees, or other resources if they are reached effectively. There are a number of such groups to which the nonprofit must market.

Customers, Clients, and Consumers

Who They Are.   Traditional marketing is reflected in an organization's efforts to seek individuals or groups to buy or consume their products and services. These individuals generally form one of the primary groups an organization will seek to satisfy.

Why They Are Important.   Obviously, if the offering is not well utilized, the organization's survival is threatened; in some cases, revenue flows directly from utilization. No organization can be successful in fulfilling its mission if it is unable to reach those it is in business to serve.

What Motivates Them.   The group's specific motivations are as diverse as the offerings of the nonprofit organization but generally can be assumed to be related to the wants and needs the nonprofit exists to serve. The organization's marketing efforts will be more effective if it understands why people are motivated toward its offerings.

Corporations and Foundations

Who They Are.   Many nonprofit organizations have developed sophisticated programs to identify and solicit funds from promising corporate and foundation sources. Corporations and foundations vary in their philanthropic interests, with many giving primarily or exclusively to focused groups such as the arts, health care, or social service.

Why They Are Important.   One of the major advantages of nonprofit status is the ability to solicit tax-deductible funds, and often large amounts of money can flow from a single corporate or foundation source. As experienced fundraisers will attest, the organization must be able to sell itself effectively in order to obtain charitable funds.

What Motivates Them.   A solid proposal that outlines the need and the organization's means of meeting that need is a traditional tool for obtaining funds, and the foundation or corporation often will seek a proposal that does not duplicate services available elsewhere in the community. However, experienced fundraisers also are aware of the "political" connections, such as personal contacts with insiders that will not hurt the foundation or corporation's motivation to give.

Individual Donors

Who They Are.   Individual donors virtually can be anyone. Although we might be tempted to assume that upper-income individuals are the most generous, some studies have indicated that those of the lower-income level are more likely to make charitable donations. A child putting a quarter in the offering plate at church is a donor, as is the billionaire writing a check for megabucks.

Why They Are Important.   There is strength in numbers, and a large donor base provides for future security for the organization. An annual appeal can raise a significant dollar amount through various donations. In addition, wealthy individual donors can be cultivated to provide major support for the organization and its programs.

What Motivates Them.   Motivations vary and may include such factors as gratitude for past services rendered, fear of contracting a disease for which research is being conducted, or a memorial for a loved one. Even though some attraction to the organization's cause exists, a personal appeal from a fundraiser to a friend or acquaintance may yield a donation for a cause in which the donor otherwise has little interest.

Government Funders

Who They Are.   Local, state, and federal government agencies frequently provide funds to nonprofit organizations, sometimes through contracts or contingent upon meeting specified standards and conditions. These agencies provide funding for causes, such as mental health, education, social service, and cultural enrichment.

Why They Are Important.   Many nonprofits largely depend on funding from government agencies as a primary source of support, and others provide additional services or programs with this funding. In some cases, these government funds are the only ones available for providing services to those who are unable to pay for them. Without government funding, these organizations would fold or be forced to compete for a shrinking pool of funds from other sources.

What Motivates Them.   Theoretically government funds are targeted toward assisting the greatest needs and enriching society; however, many a nonprofit manager would say that the political climate is an important, or even the sole, determiner of government funding. Issues that are "hot" and capture the attention of voters may receive the most government funds.

Volunteers

Who They Are.   Volunteers come from all segments of society, including welfare recipients who work to make their subsidized housing safer and upper-income individuals who work at the hospital or the conservatory one afternoon per week. As the pool of stay-at-home women shrinks, other groups are being targeted to pick up the slack in the volunteer workforce.

Why They Are Important.   As the volunteer workforce dwindles, the nonprofit faces the need to market itself effectively to the prospective volunteer, concentrating on attracting and retaining a dynamic pool of workers. Some nonprofit offerings depend on a pool of volunteers to the extent that they would be unable to exist without that support.

What Motivates Them.   Volunteers come with their own wants and needs that the organization must recognize in order to attract and retain them. Even altruism reflects the satisfaction of a personal desire to feel useful and to contribute to society. Volunteers also may seek social contact, eventual paid employment, professional advancement, or enjoyment. In nearly all cases, volunteers appreciate recognition for their gift of time.

Board Members

Who They Are.   Board membership varies with the type of organization. Some organizations make an effort to achieve diversity with variables such as age, sex, race, and religion. Others recruit board members because of their ability to contribute needed skills in areas such as finance or marketing. Some organizations seek individuals with power and wealth who represent the area's "old money." In any case, board members should be selected to meet certain criteria and specific needs.

Why They Are Important.   Excellent organizations often have excellent board members, who give freely of their work, wealth, and wisdom. Many organizations have developed sophisticated plans to identify, approach, and recruit tomorrow's leaders. In addition, the wise organization will attend to the wants and needs of strong board leaders to continue their involvement.

What Motivates Them.   As a special category of volunteers, board members' motivations can vary widely and can include a sincere interest in a cause, a desire to make contacts and "network" with others, or the need to learn new skills. These and other motivations should be recognized in order to match individuals with responsibilities and ensure that the experience motivates members to stay and contribute.

Referral Agents

Who They Are.   In many cases, individuals or organizations make referrals. A family physician may suggest counseling or social services, and one social service agency may refer clients to another that provides additional, specialized services, such as housing, educational, financial assistance, or health care.

Why They Are Important.   Other individuals or organizations can be effective marketers for the nonprofit if the referral relationship is carefully developed and nourished. Often, organizations prosper by building referral networks, finding that this attracts appropriate consumers without the costs of direct consumer marketing.

What Motivates Them.   Ideally, referrals are made in the best interest of the consumer; the referral agent recognizes a want or need and suggests the organization as a source of fulfillment. This, of course, is based upon the referring agency's knowledge and respect of the organization's work. However, other motivations come into play as well, such as personal or professional connections between the referral source and the organization to which the referral is made.

Significant Others

Who They Are.   The families, friends, and loved ones of clients form an important group that nonprofits should consider. They often are the first line of contact for the organization.

Why They Are Important.   In some cases, decisions regarding services are not made by the direct consumer. Families and friends may play a major role in making choices for clients, such as for children, the frail elderly, and the mentally impaired. In other cases, they will be important influences through word-of-mouth marketing and well-intentioned referrals for services. The nonprofit organization must reach out to these significant others and provide needed information and encouragement.

What Motivates Them.   The significant others, one would hope, are motivated by a sincere concern for the welfare and enrichment of the potential client, attempting to match wants and needs with the appropriate organization that will meet them. Significant others also are motivated by their own needs, as they seek assistance in dealing with a problem child, an elderly relative, or an addicted spouse.

Employees

Who They Are.   The employees of nonprofit organizations range from unskilled laborers who clean the restrooms to high-powered executives who command six-figure salaries. The collective efforts of many individuals are needed in order to carry out the organization's work.

Why They Are Important.   Many nonprofit organizations have difficulty in attracting and retaining skilled, qualified employees for a number of reasons. Salary scales may be low compared to those of private industry, discouraging longevity even among those who enjoy their work. Professional groups with specific qualifications, such as nurses, teachers, or therapists, may be in short supply. Often, the organization will find itself needing a plan to recruit and keep staff.

What Motivates Them.   Like any employee, the nonprofit worker seeks fulfillment, responsibility, decent wages, benefits, and favorable working conditions. At times, the mission of the organization is a motivating factor, because employees believe in the organization's cause and serve with a personal commitment. Attention to employee wants and needs is important especially in low-budget organizations where financial incentives are lacking.

MARKETING TO THE ORGANIZATION'S IMPORTANT GROUPS

Remember our definition of marketing from chapter one. The effective nonprofit marketer will seek to apply each of these steps in a comprehensive marketing approach:

• **A means of identifying what is wanted and needed.** The nonprofit must understand the motivations of each group, which obviously will differ greatly. A board member may be seeking resumé enhancement, yet the employee may be interested in security and a good pension. The volunteer may want recognition, and the client, a sympathetic ear. In each of these cases, the wants and needs must be recognized, and the organization must work toward their satisfaction in order to attain the benefits the group offers.

• **A mechanism for bringing together an individual or group that has wants or needs with an individual or group that can satisfy those wants or needs.** The organization's success depends upon attracting members of all the groups mentioned above and more. In order to succeed, it is necessary to develop mechanisms for marketing to each of these target groups separately, convincing them that this organization has the means to satisfy their wants and needs.

• **A focus on understanding and serving the client, customer, or consumer.** Continuing to provide for the wants and needs of the target group is important for ongoing success. Many organizations supply this with volunteer banquets, employee appreciation events, board recognition of various types, good service, and a caring spirit in all they do.

Without a marketing approach to important groups, the organization will find that it is struggling to maintain the status quo and will not be able to attract and retain the resources needed to run the organization. However, the marketing approach to each of these groups can differ greatly.

For example, a nonprofit organization offers health care, social services, and educational services to low-income pregnant, teens. They need to attract:

Consumers, the teens in need of services. These teens must be reached and made to feel comfortable in seeking the agency's services.

Funding from corporations and foundations. Proposals must be prepared and the funder courted through personal contacts and a meritorious proposal.

Individual donors. A prospect list and appropriate appeals must be developed in order to gain support.

Government funders. The organization must understand the system and how funding is granted in order to receive assistance.

Volunteers. A volunteer workforce is needed in order to carry out the program and serve clients.

Board. Committed board members who are willing to provide governance as well as assistance are needed.

Referral agents. Other agencies that provide social and health care services will channel appropriate referrals.

Significant others. The families and friends of the pregnant teen may be important sources of information and advice.

Employees. The organization must attract and retain professionals, such as nurses, who are in short supply, as well as contend with a salary scale that provides little financial reward.

The wants, needs, and the means of approaching these groups must be tailored to their characteristics, wants, and needs. Marketing one program to many different groups requires a different approach for each group. Multiply the number of programs or services by the number of groups the organization must reach and that figure will illustrate the complexity of the marketing campaign for the organization.

SEGMENTING AND TARGETING THE MARKET

Realistically, the nonprofit organization cannot be all things to all people. The organization must decide whom it will serve and in what way; this decision is central to its statement of mission as well as to its efforts in resource attraction and resource allocation.

In chapter one, we explored the way nonprofit organizations usually market services, experiences, products, concepts, and the organization itself. Just as each offering requires diverse marketing tasks, people differ as well. In order to carry out the marketing process, to understand wants and needs, to reach consumers, and to ensure satisfaction, the organization must know exactly who those potential consumers are and how best to appeal to them.

There are two important processes for dividing potential individuals or groups into smaller subgroups.

• **Segmenting** describes the activity of dividing a market or potential market into meaningful subgroups. People are divided into these groups for a number of practical reasons. Needs and wants may be similar among the members of the group, and differ from those of other groups. The organization might more effectively carry out the marketing process by recognizing these different groups. The processes of identifying wants and needs, reaching out and ensuring satisfaction may be more effective when the nonprofit recognizes that different types of people have different types of needs.

• **Targeting** indicates that the organization chooses to appeal to, market to, or create offerings for one or more identified segments of the market. Clearly, an organization with limited resources must choose the segments it will target. Targeting is important in the organization's decision making regarding mission and marketing; leaders must determine the target groups and how best to reach and serve them.

Segmenting and targeting are processes that help an organization pinpoint activities and organize efforts. Let's look at an example:

> Seniors Providing Service is an organization that works with people over the age of sixty who volunteer their time and expertise to the community. The organization is planning its volunteer recruitment strategy for·the coming year and is beginning by examining internal data on the number and types of volunteers already in service. It also is tracking external data such as demographics and geographics regarding senior citizens in the area. The organization has identified several major types or segments of their group of volunteers:
> - Retired executives or professionals—this group may be predominantly male and possess the desire to pass along their knowledge and expertise to younger business managers. They seek volunteer opportunities in professional settings.
> - Retired homemakers—women whose career has been raising a family and maintaining a home, many of whom no longer have extended families in the area and feel lonely and unfulfilled. They may want opportunities to work with children or young mothers.
> - Lonely widows and widowers—men and women who are coping with the loss of a spouse and are seeking opportunities to interact with others and to feel that they are productive, useful members of society.

These groups are segmented on several important demographic characteristics, such as gender, professional or occupational background and marital status, and in many cases share common wants and needs that should be addressed in order to retain their volunteer services. Following this segmentation, the board and managers of Seniors Providing Service examine the needs of the community and determine that there are many latchkey children and local preschools needing workers to interact with their young students. The organization decides that its next recruitment campaign should have one primary target: the retired homemaker segment of the volunteer workforce. As a result, the following actions are taken:

- Posters and flyers promoting volunteer opportunities are placed in senior centers where a high percentage of the participants are members of the target group.
- A feature story is published in the local newspaper emphasizing the important role of older homemakers in working with children through the organization and the resulting fulfillment.
- Staff and volunteers speak to church, civic, and other organizations that have women members who are targeted for recruitment.

- Existing volunteers are asked to spread the word to their friends and acquaintances about the organization and its good work.

These tactics are deliberate efforts to target one segment of the market for this organization. Often, the promotional efforts may increase public awareness of the activities in other areas and create a spillover effect into other programs. Importantly, the organization has identified subgroups within the volunteer workforce, established priorities, and created a plan for recruitment of that segment.

FACTORS FOR SEGMENTATION AND TARGETING

There are a number of factors involved in determining how the organization can subdivide its important groups. Some are fairly obvious, universal distinctions among people, but others might be unique to the organization and the population it serves. The following represents a few of the ways a market might be segmented.

Demographics

Demographic segmentation divides the market into groups that have in common one or more sets of characteristics. A few examples:

Age.   Children and adults can have different wants and needs in areas such as mental health services, education, entertainment, and healthcare. Young adults and older adults can need different services as well. Age is a common characteristic on which to segment, since members of an age group share common characteristics and needs.

Sex.   Gender is an obvious characteristic that differentiates people. Clearly, only women directly utilize obstetric and gynecological services, and men are the exclusive market for vasectomies. Aside from these physiological differences, there are many characteristics that presumably separate the sexes. Women traditionally have been the decision makers concerning childcare and family health matters; men are thought to have a greater focus on investments and financial security. However, as rigid sex roles blur, gender segmentation may become somewhat less useful.

Education.   The amount and type of education an individual has had may indicate a number of characteristics for that individual. For example, people who are college educated are likely to share some interests and characteristics, including attendance at artistic performances, enrollment of their children in extracurricular or advanced educational activities, and interest in educational television. Those with little education most likely will be targets for programs dealing with literacy, high school equivalency, and early childhood enrichment programs.

Racial, Ethnic, or Religious Group Membership.   Some nonprofit organizations exist, exclusively or primarily, to serve the needs of a specific ethnic, religious, or racial group. These nonprofits might include social organizations for persons of a certain nationality, groups that work to advance the status of minorities that have been the victims of discrimination or organizations interested in the culture and traditions of a specific ethnic segment. Churches target current or potential members of their religion for membership, donations, and volunteer services.

Segmentation and targeting by race, ethnicity, or religion can be useful for organizations with wide constituencies as well. Many nonprofits seek to expand their reach by achieving a better balance on their board and by recruiting members of groups that have been underrepresented. The organization also might seek to serve communities with high percentages of individuals from certain ethnic, racial, and religious groups, and this knowledge can be valuable in planning the marketing approach.

Geographics

Some organizations have large service areas: an example is an organization that serves hungry persons in a number of third world nations. Another organization may be formed to serve the interests of a small neighborhood. Therefore, geographic segmentation may be a matter of mission, focusing on the needs of people within a specific region. However, segmentation and targeting also can be a matter of discretion, such as the addition of a new program that will primarily, but not exclusively, serve the residents of a section of the city because of demonstrated need there. People also are segmented geographically because of common cultural characteristics that exist in that region—for example, residents of a small midwestern town are thought to differ from the residents of a large east coast city.

Psychographics

There is another area in which people differ that is perhaps the most significant of all—the area of psychographics. Psychographics attempts to group people by their attitudes, beliefs, and psychological characteristics, which often coincide with other accompanying attributes. The following is an example of a psychographic portrait:

The designation "yuppie" is a psychographic description. These individuals are not merely members of an age or income category, but
also may share other, less tangible characteristics, such as an interest
in career advancement, material acquisition, and less interest in philanthropic giving. We visualize a yuppie wearing a well-tailored suit
or brand-name leisure clothing, living in a fashionable suburb, and
driving a luxury car complete with car phone.

A psychographic portrait such as this one gives us information on the
marketing efforts that most likely will be effective in reaching a group.
We can better understand their motivations, their lifestyle, and how they
might be reached. For example, having a high-income, high-status board
member contact a yuppie concerning joining the board might be more
effective than having a suburban homemaker call; this will appeal to the
desire for status and achievement.

Wants and Needs

People can be divided into categories based on their wants and
needs. This is a practical and useful way of dividing a population for
many organizations. For example:

- Students may be average, gifted, learning disabled, or retarded.
- Mental health clients seek services for mood disorders, cognitive disorders, adjustment problems, and family dysfunction.
- Women contact the family planning agency for gynecological
  care, birth control, or assistance with unplanned preg-
  nancies.
- A cancer support program serves families, recovering individuals, and the terminally ill.
- Music lovers prefer rock, soul, classical, or jazz.

These examples show that nonprofits can serve many different needs,
and that segmenting and targeting the population as a whole on the
basis of wants and needs can make sense. In planning and offering
services and in reaching and satisfying target markets, the organization
that recognizes that wants and needs differ from person to person and
that a different marketing approach is needed will be in a better position
to carry out an effective marketing program.

MARKETING IN A MULTICULTURAL SOCIETY

Marketing in the nonprofit organization is both interesting and challenging in a multicultural society. Race, religion, or ethnicity are factors
that frequently are cited as forming the basis of culture. Defined broadly,

we might see a number of different groups, each with its own unique "minority culture" and relating to the "majority culture" with which it must coexist.

The highly charged multicultural society in which we live provides a difficult challenge, since the organization must seek to understand and market its offerings to many different segments of society. Some organizations have as their mission dealing with a specific culture, such as serving Spanish-speaking children, providing counseling in a Christian framework, or working to end discrimination against specific minorities. Other organizations have a broad scope, such as a library serving everyone in a geographic area or a program that works with victims of heart disease. In either case, there is a need to be sensitive to the cultural diversity and its implications.

Characteristics of a culture such as a strong reliance on the church or the extended family are important to understand when fulfilling the organization's mission. In addition, the organization should recognize the barriers that must be overcome, such as a mistrust of outsiders, a belief that problems should be solved within the family, or a reluctance to separate from others of the same culture in order to take positive advantage of what the world has to offer.

Although some businesses are criticized for attempting to exploit targeted cultural groups, nonprofits are in an excellent position to take advantage of a knowledge of and sensitivity to cultural factors in a positive manner. In the marketing process, the organization's charge to identify, reach, and satisfy those it exists to serve will be carried out more effectively by incorporating an understanding and respect of individuals of all cultures into the standard operating procedure.

THE DANGERS OF SEGMENTATION

Oversimplification in the development and use of market segmentation can be counterproductive and can even result in offensive stereotyping if used improperly. It should be clear that although there may be some similarities among groups, there are important differences as well.

Although it often is appropriate to segment the market based on a characteristic such as race or sex, the marketer must keep in mind that not all members of a segment are alike. Women, for example, differ in regard to their age, education, socioeconomic status, whether they work outside the home or have children. Assuming that women are all family oriented and will respond to pink brochures is as erroneous as assuming that all minorities are underprivileged or that all young professionals are greedy and materialistic.

Even though segmentation provides some clues regarding the characteristics of the market, it should not be seen as a marketing panacea. Looking at combinations of characteristics will give a better clue to the true nature of the group; for example, young professional women with preschool children who reside in the northern suburbs of the city may share a number of characteristics, wants, and needs. The more refined and detailed the effort at segmentation and targeting, the more useful the activity likely is to be.

HOW THE NONPROFIT FACES MARKETING CHALLENGES

This chapter has addressed some of the important groups to which the organization must market and has outlined the complexity of marketing the nonprofit organization. The organization has many groups to consider for even a single service and program. This can easily translate into a marketing nightmare, which the organization is ill-prepared to face.

Although later in the book we will discuss the issues of marketing plans and the marketing workforce, it is important to realize that few organizations even attempt formal plans to deal with each of these constituent groups. With limited resources, it is important to prioritize and tackle each marketing issue to the fullest extent.

Unfortunately, some organizations fail to recognize the number of important groups with different characteristics and the importance of identifying their wants and needs, reaching out to them, and working toward their satisfaction.

REVIEW QUESTIONS

1. What is meant by resource attraction and resource allocation?
2. What is the role of resource attraction in each of the following types of programs: resource consuming, partially self-supporting, breakeven, and profitable?
3. What are some of the major groups to which the nonprofit must market?
4. What are some of the motivations that must be considered among these major groups?
5. What is meant by segmenting and targeting the market?
6. Of what practical value are segmenting and targeting?
7. On what characteristics can the market be segmented?
8. What are the risks and dangers associated with segmentation?
9. Why are social trends important in understanding target groups?
10. Do most organizations seek to develop comprehensive marketing programs for each subgroup of their markets? Why or why not?

MINI CASE STUDY

Landmark Museum is located in a medium-sized city and houses both art and natural history collections. Attendance has fallen off, particularly during the weekdays, and this is causing concern. Landmark is aware that other museums have offered special programs for identified groups of potential visitors and is wondering if that approach might work.

Its board and management staff is interested in developing a marketing plan to increase the number of visitors to the museum, as well as sales of souvenirs and items available in the gift shop. They have studied the external environment and have learned that the area recently has attracted a number of young people, both singles and married couples with young children. However, its records show that many current attendees are middle-aged or elderly persons who have resided in the area for many years. The leadership of Landmark is eager to apply marketing principles to improve its situation.

1. What important groups must the museum consider in its marketing efforts?
2. How might visitors to the museum be segmented?
3. What sort of social trends might affect the number and type of museum attendees?
4. What groups might be targets for new museum programs and promotional efforts?

FURTHER READING

Andreasen, Alan R. Nonprofits: Check Your Attention to Customers. *Harvard Business Review,* May–June 1982, 105–10, vol. 60, no. 3.

Espy, Siri N. Keep the Customer Satisfied. *Nonprofit World,* 5(4): July/August 1987, p. 35.

———. *Handbook of Strategic Planning for Nonprofit Organizations.* New York: Praeger Publishers, 1986.

Kotler, Philip. *Marketing for Nonprofit Organizations.* Englewood Cliffs, NJ: Prentice-Hall, 1982.

CHAPTER 4

Environmental and Internal Analyses in Marketing

The Birthing Center was founded to be an innovative and responsive source for families seeking a warm, homelike atmosphere for childbirth. However, three years later the director finds herself wondering how to react to changes in the organization and environment so the center can remain as client centered as its founders intended. As she sits at her desk, she looks down at two stacks of paper—one details the operating statistics of the center for the past year, and the other consists of population projections and articles about national trends affecting the birthrate and attitudes and preferences of expectant parents. She contemplates many factors, including decreased utilization of the center, a rising number of women over thirty giving birth, and increased competition by hospitals that offer comfortable birthing suites. She thinks the Birthing Center will need to examine these trends and figure out what they mean.

Many nonprofit organizations are trying to function in what seems like a topsy-turvy world. Reliable funding sources are drying up, competition is intensifying for all types of resources, and the face of the nonprofit consumer is changing. Trusted ally organizations are stealing innovative ideas, and new alliances are forming. The organization's resources are being allocated differently, and the characteristics of its workforce are changing. The population is older and more transient than it once was, and national demographics are shifting. What's a poor nonprofit organization to do?

Keeping up with changes both inside and outside the organization is a major challenge for today's nonprofit. Even a modest goal of maintaining the status quo can require a heavy commitment of resources in a rapidly changing environment. The organization that knows and understands trends will have additional weapons in a war of survival. Those who lack up-to-date information about the worlds inside and outside the organization will be slow to respond to important changes and therefore less able to fulfill the mission for which they exist.

THE IMPORTANCE OF DATA

Many managers brag that their decision making is done by "gut feeling," only to discover later that the feeling was gas followed by severe indigestion when the ramifications of that gut decision making come to light. In order to carry on an effective marketing program, the nonprofit organization must rely on the best data available. Granted, data may be imperfect, unreliable, or erroneous, and we all know that data can be used to support nearly any desired conclusion. But there are some comforts as well as some occasional surprises when data are collected, analyzed, and interpreted well.

Data can be used to look at current conditions, as in statistics regarding the utilization of a specific program or an organization's balance sheet. These data can be helpful as a starting point, but in order to get the complete picture it is important to look at the historical or trend data available to the organization. A sharp downturn or an uptick in performance may be temporary and easily explained, but it also can signal the end for a program or service or the beginning of a whole new era. Looking at the trends tells us not only where we are today, but where we've been and are likely to go.

Sad to say, but even the most sophisticated data gathering and analysis yields imperfect results. There is no such thing as perfect, complete information in the real world, in which no variables are controlled and every day essentially is a crapshoot. Unanticipated changes occur, clandestine arrangements come to light, and people behave in unforeseen ways. The bad news, then, is that management decision making always is conducted with incomplete information and carried out with varying degrees of risk. The good news is that the bad news carries with it a perpetual need for imperfect human managers to practice the art of management using the best available information.

INTERNAL AND EXTERNAL DATA

Information that is available and needed to make decisions in an organization can be thought of as internal or external in nature. Internal and external data both are important in conducting a thorough market analysis.

Internal data describe the organization itself and give information regarding its operation. External data describe the environment in which the organization operates. Table 4-1 shows a few examples.

The first step in any journey is knowing where you are now. Data,

TABLE 4-1   Information Available and Needed for Decision Making

Internal Data	External Data
Financial statements	Giving patterns of Americans
Utilization statistics	Population demographics
Staffing patterns	Reports on technological developments
Salary scales	Economic trends
Donation records	Attitude studies
Program evaluation data	Expert opinions on trends

such as those described above, will help you in pinpointing your present standing as well as in projecting some trends. Perhaps you will see patterns in the internal data that suggest the direction your organization is headed, or secondary data will contain projections and educated guesses regarding trends in your field. Pulling together available internal data as well as reviewing published literature and other external data will help obtain a thorough, accurate picture of the environment in which the organization operates.

INTERNAL ANALYSIS

The internal analysis of an organization might take many forms and may be a simple or complex task depending on the sophistication of the organization and the amount of information available. In any case, an internal analysis is designed to yield valuable information regarding the organization and its operations.

A good place to start is with historical data. Although an organization founded in the last century may not need to include records from its early days, it is important to get a sense of where the organization has been.

An internal analysis might include information about factors such as the following:

- Financial stability
- Donations and grants
- Program utilization
- Staff capability
- Volunteer preferences
- Community group representation on the board of directors
- Budgets of various programs and departments
- Staffing patterns
- Amount of publicity received per year
- Client satisfaction measures

Profiles of factors such as these can show the progress the organization has made on its way to the present situation. Looking at the ups and downs of such data will give some idea of the elements of past successes and failures for use in planning and marketing programs in the future.

In the nonprofit, evaluation is not always as easy as charting numbers since the mission tends to be complex and multifaceted. Therefore, an internal analysis also can include qualitative as well as quantitative information, evaluating various successes and failures in fulfilling the mission and meeting the needs of various stakeholder groups.

An internal analysis helps in learning from the past as well as in predicting the future. In many cases, a decline in funding, volunteers, or program utilization can foretell difficult times ahead. Looking at past failures can provide clues for needed modifications for future offerings. Like working a jigsaw puzzle, a thorough internal analysis represents the process of putting together the pieces of a complex picture that is the organization.

Nonprofits rather uniquely are driven by the values of their founders and stakeholders. No internal analysis can be complete without exploring those factors and their implications. Corporate values and culture in the organization are difficult to quantify, yet in many cases they represent the dimension on which the organization differentiates itself from all others. As a result, the wants and needs of those who operate and govern the organization are reflected in the climate, beliefs, and resulting modus operandi of the nonprofit organization. These influences are as strong as or stronger than factors in the marketplace. The organization will decide what it wants to be and will sacrifice financial and competitive success and a glitzy image to do so.

The nonprofit manager must face the difficult task of ferreting out the values and beliefs of those within the organization. Working to develop a statement of vision, philosophy, or values can help the organization clarify these unique values that will help to set the parameters of the organization's efforts.

PRIMARY VS. SECONDARY DATA

Data can be classified according to source: primary or secondary. Primary data are collected by the organization according to its own procedures and for its own purposes. Secondary data have been collected by one person or one organization and are available for use by a second organization.

Primary data include information such as the following:

- Market research carried out by the organization or done under contract with that organization by a research firm
- Program data, including utilization and financial statistics
- Customer satisfaction survey results
- Records of giving patterns by donor classification

Secondary data are plentiful and readily available to determined and knowledgeable seekers. Public and university libraries and social and government agencies contain volumes of data regarding just about everything. Reference librarians often are well trained in locating and retrieving a wealth of information on a variety of topics.

Secondary data include:

- Census data, which enumerate and describe the population in a specific geographic area
- Market research conducted and published by another organization
- Demographic data and projections gathered by government and planning agencies
- Psychological studies describing the characteristics of a certain group of people

ADVANTAGES AND DISADVANTAGES OF PRIMARY AND SECONDARY DATA

There are times when primary data are needed in order to supply the organization with relevant, valid information. However, secondary data also can be useful and descriptive. The marketer, then, needs to know how to proceed in gathering and using data. Table 4-2 describes some of the major advantages and disadvantages of primary and secondary data.

Any organization that hopes to develop a well-focused marketing

TABLE 4-2   Major Advantages and Disadvantages of Primary vs. Secondary Data

Primary Data	
Advantages	*Disadvantages*
Custom tailored to answer a specific question or set of questions	Conducting custom studies can be expensive
Known, reliable methodology	There typically is a time delay between recognizing the need for data and completing the study
The organization has more control over the gathering and use of the data	Data must be gathered by skilled, competent personnel in order to be valid

Secondary Data	
Advantages	*Disadvantages*
Available free or at a reasonable cost	Quality and reliability generally is uncertain
Quickly obtainable when the need is recognized	Originally gathered for one purpose—may not be easily generalized to another situation
Limited expertise is needed to obtain and interpret	Source may be outdated
May be collected by highly skilled, sophisticated researchers	Conclusions drawn may be invalid

program will need to weigh the advantages and disadvantages of primary and secondary data. Often the budgetary constraints under which most nonprofits labor will be the deciding factor in favor of "making do" with the best available secondary data, supplemented with the limited primary data the organization can muster. Sending someone to the library to poke around and calling a few government agencies or other organizations can yield an impressive array of data, on which a number of conclusions can be based.

Clearly, there is no simple answer to meeting our need for data. Some secondary data, such as census findings, often are used to draw conclusions about the population of a certain area and probably are the best, most complete estimates available in many cases. Many of the interim projections and conclusions drawn about a population are based on the last census, as well. These data, although often the best guess, carry certain flaws such as imperfect collection methodologies and fading accuracy as the decade progresses and the demographics of an area change. This especially is true in areas where inmigration or outmigration of significant proportions have occurred or where a major change, such as the collapse or growth of a regional industry, has occurred.

ENVIRONMENTAL SCANNING

One of the most crucial tasks for any organization is keeping up with the world around it. Attempting to offer products and services that do not respond to the current wants and needs of a potential clientele will place the organization in a poor position for the future. There are a number of trends in the environment that dictate what business the organization is in and how it must conduct its business in order to survive and prosper.

Monitoring environmental trends is a task that can be accomplished by any organization, even one with modest resources. A trip to the library to review published literature, reading and clipping local and national publications, and maintaining files of the brochures and printed material of competing organizations are simple ways to start scanning the environment in which the organization operates.

The first step for many organizations might be identifying some of the important trends that affect its operations and are likely to affect it in the future. Let's look at some of these trends and why they are important to the nonprofit organization.

Economic Trends

The economic environment in which the organization operates will play a major part in determining what services are wanted and needed in the area. Economic data to be tracked include factors such as:

- Unemployment rates
- Per capita and household income
- Buying power
- Buying patterns
- Inflation rates
- Interest rates
- Housing prices

These and other economic indicators describe the overall financial health of areas of interest to the organization and provide it with a great deal of valuable information. Economic data help the organization make decisions about its operation such as:

- A prosperous community might be a source of donors and volunteers and might support the arts, education, and child enrichment activities.
- An economically disadvantaged area requires social services to support basic wants and needs and can not support services and experiences that require discretionary income.
- High housing prices may lead to increased homelessness and lower income families seeking subsidized housing.
- High unemployment rates in an area indicate a need for job placement and basic assistance services.

Political Trends

Political changes can be precursors to legislative and regulatory changes. Who gets elected and how they perceive the value of the organization and its work can be of great importance to the nonprofit organization. The philosophies or platforms of political candidates can address important issues, such as:

- Abortion
- Child care
- Social service budgets
- Mental health/mental retardation appropriations
- Support for the arts
- Programs for the elderly

An organization that tracks such factors can work to support candidates who will be sympathetic to its causes and can anticipate the changes that are likely to result from the election of a particular candidate or administration. Monitoring political developments can help an organization plan for many eventualities, such as:

- Working to counter the pro-choice or pro-life position of an elected candidate by garnering public support for the cause
- Preparing for program cutbacks so they can be well-planned instead of last-minute and haphazard
- Preparing for program expansions in areas where increased appropriations are likely

Legal/Regulatory Trends

Many nonprofit organizations are to some degree at the mercy of legislative or regulatory bodies, which can change the way the organization operates or the business it pursues. Some examples of legal and regulatory trends that nonprofits may want to monitor include:

- Changes in the tax laws regarding charitable deductions
- New regulations that have an impact on the type and number of personnel needed to provide services
- Efforts to challenge the tax-exempt status of nonprofit organizations
- Accreditation standards that increase the need for documentation
- Medicare and Medicaid regulations that affect health care reimbursement

Recognizing these factors early on is important for several reasons. First, the organization may be able to band together with others and attempt to affect decisions before they are made or work to change laws or regulations that have been enacted. Also, the organization that anticipates upcoming changes is in a better position to adapt and plan for dealing with the change in the best way possible, for example:

- An organization may want to launch a public information campaign about its truly charitable nature to counter challenges to tax exemption.
- Advance staff training might be needed to ensure a workforce that is competent to meet upcoming changes in the regulations.
- Marketing plans may need to be adjusted to attract a better mix of paying consumers in light of upcoming Medicare cuts.

Technological Trends

Technological changes have been staggeringly rapid within the past few decades, and in many cases, have had an impact on society, the economy, and other areas as well. New technologies that might affect the nonprofit organization include:

- Computerization of many record-keeping functions
- Fax machines
- Life-prolonging medical procedures
- New drugs that improve the quality of life
- Computerized psychotherapy
- Computer-aided teaching methods for children with mental or physical limitations
- New techniques to combat infertility
- Safe, effective methods of birth control

These and many other developments affect the way many nonprofit organizations do business, making life easier and more difficult for the nonprofit manager.

Some of the changes that technology might bring to the nonprofit include:

- Longer-term survival for those with diseases, changing the organization's mission from support for dying to support for living with the disease
- Babies with serious or chronic medical problems as a result of surviving premature birth
- The need for computer-literate workers or training for existing staff
- A change in the structure of society itself with birth rates declining due to abortion and birth control, and life spans increasing due to medical advances

Social Trends

Social changes have been rapid and pervasive in our society. Some may be seen as positive, and others are viewed as the beginning of the end for our civilization as we know it—the distinction is in the eye of the beholder.

Social changes include:

- More single-parent families
- Higher numbers of women in the workforce

- Increased openness about alternative lifestyles
- High divorce rates
- Drug abuse among all socioeconomic groups

The impact of social changes on nonprofits is obvious. No organization can expect to stay in business and fulfill its mission if it fails to recognize and keep up with social changes. A number of social factors might indicate a change in the way the organization will do business, such as:

- With more women working outside the home, there is an increased need to provide care for both children and the elderly.
- More counseling and support groups for single parents and stepfamilies are needed.
- Drug abuse treatment is needed not only in slum areas, but among white collar workers and top executives.
- Organizations that support the rights of stigmatized groups such as gays are becoming more prominent and vocal.

Demographic Trends

Demographic trends clearly signal changes in the market for non-profit offerings. These changes may be national in scope, or they might affect only one small area. In any case, they are worth tracking and noting as the nonprofit works to fulfill its mission.

Demographic changes might include:

- An increase or decrease in the number of residents in a geographic area
- A change in the average household income
- The graying of America, which may be magnified in some communities
- Increased or decreased birthrates
- Changes in the type of residents attracted to a community

These changes indicate some fundamental realities about the area served by a nonprofit. This will have implications for the nonprofit in a number of ways:

- A community that attracts or retains older residents but few young people will need senior centers and services.
- An area that is undergoing significant growth and development might be a target for satellite clinics aimed at an upscale clientele.

- High birthrates will indicate an interest in daycare and nursery school programs.
- A community that is attracting more, or less, affluent residents will support different types of programs and offerings.

THE IMPORTANCE OF ENVIRONMENTAL SCANNING

It should be clear by this point that the organization has a great deal of work to do in identifying and tracking important environmental trends. Unfortunately, ignoring even one important development can cost the organization significant opportunities for growth and make it vulnerable to threats. Let's look at one example:

> Blue Valley Hospital is located in an area that has undergone significant change in the last decade. Many of the younger residents in its primary service area have moved away to seek better jobs, creating a predominantly elderly community. The area has become less affluent as the potential wage earners leave. Blue Valley has experienced a significant increase in Medicare and Medicaid patients as a result, which has had a negative impact on its financial bottom line. In addition, efforts to expand the hospital have met with criticism from local elected officials, who fear that the tax base will be further eroded by more tax-exempt property.
>
> Several neighboring communities, however, are faring better. They are experiencing growth and development and attracting younger families with higher incomes and birthrates. More residences and businesses are moving to these outlying communities, to which Blue Valley has never made a significant effort to market and attract patients.

The implications for Blue Valley Hospital are several. It is facing an unfavorable demographic, economic, political, and regulatory climate in its primary service area. Efforts to recruit physicians and new patients in the neighboring area might be expanded, with several advantages: more affluent patients will lead to a better payer mix, a growing population will be a source of new patients, and the neighboring areas might be amenable to the location of office buildings or health centers operated by the hospital.

These demographic changes indicate the need for a new approach because Blue Valley Hospital will need to be certain that its offerings in areas such as obstetrics and pediatrics prove attractive to the residents of the neighboring area. New marketing efforts will be needed to increase awareness and market penetration in this new area, and the hospital will need to examine its competitors in that area and determine how it will serve the needs of the residents well enough to attract new business.

Recognizing changes in the external environment, then, will give the organization a head start in planning for the changing times ahead. Blue Valley Hospital and organizations like it will face a grim future if they are unable to recognize and respond to change before it threatens survival.

EXAMINING THE IMPACT OF ENVIRONMENTAL TRENDS

Many nonprofit organizations have discovered that changes in the world around them have produced marked changes in the services they must provide. The application of information gathered in the environmental scanning process will assist the organization in understanding the world around it and how its important groups are changing. Each organization must examine these trends in terms of their importance to programs and services and then project their impact to plan for the future. Let's look at several of those changes and some of their implications:

Trend: **Women entering the workforce in larger numbers**

Implications: Increased need for child care
Elder care is needed
Shrinking volunteer workforce
Adoption of cats, which need less care than dogs
Evening and weekend hours for services
Additional stress and demands for women

Trend: **An increasing number of elderly citizens**

Implications: Additional social services needed
Additional healthcare services needed
Potential source of paid and volunteer labor
Opportunities for intergenerational programs
Marketing of existing programs to seniors

Trend: **Drug abuse that spans demographic categories**

Implications: Additional treatment facilities needed
More education needed, at a younger age
Programs for addicted infants
Treatment for white collar, upper-income groups

TYPES OF COMPETITION

When we think of competition in the marketplace, it is easy to imagine an automobile advertisement comparing the price, features, and appeal of their product with another car. In the nonprofit sector, the issue of competition often is not a straightforward one, because there can be many levels and types of competition for potential resources.

Consequently, the organization can lose these resources to a competitor at many points. Competition can be thought to take place in several arenas:

• Competition among similar organizations occurs when two organizations with comparable missions and services compete for the same resources, such as clients, volunteers, or funding. For example, two preschools are targeted to serving the same type of child in the same geographic area, or two arts organizations appeal for funding to the same group of the city's affluent and culture-minded citizens. Competitors of this type may be relatively easy to identify, because there is likely to be a limited group of directly competing organizations.

• Competition among dissimilar organizations offering similar services occurs when two or more organizations, which differ along some significant dimension, compete for resources by offering services or products that can be substituted for the nonprofit's offerings. Laboratory services, for example, might be offered in the doctor's office or the hospital lab. Here, physicians and hospitals are competing for the same healthcare dollar. A person seeking to stop smoking might look for help at a for-profit program, a hypnotist, an acupuncturist, or a program sponsored by a nonprofit concerned with the health of heart and lungs. In many cases, the nonprofit's competition consists of organizations of a different sort. It can be a difficult task to enumerate and track the actions of a number of dissimilar organizations.

• Competition among organizations, services, and offerings that seem to have little in common. A person who is seeking a pleasant weekend afternoon might opt for a baseball game, the opera, the zoo, dirt biking, a trip to the mall, a movie, or a lazy day of eating potato chips and drinking beer. Although few nonprofits would view the mall or dirt bikes as competition, in some cases consumers, revenue, and other resources are lost due to such circumstances. Enumerating and studying all such competition is virtually impossible. The organization's task in such cases is determining how to maximize its appeal.

• Inactivity can be the greatest competitor for a nonprofit. Doing nothing about a problem or situation is a frequent course of action, and the organization must work to help its constituents overcome their inertia. Potential consumers, even well-intentioned ones, may choose not to deal with a marital conflict or weight problem at all. They may have great interest in making a donation but put the solicitation aside and lose track of it. The organization must find effective ways to help motivate potential consumers to take the desired action. Some marketing campaigns directly target inactivity as a competitor, urging the public to get more exercise, learn to read, or complete high school.

An example of one organization that recognizes the importance of competition at all levels is a center for inpatient drug and alcohol rehabilitation services that will compete against other providers of inpatient treatment (direct competitors). But if the center were to examine where potential clients go for help, it might find that many are choosing outpatient services (a competitor offering a similar type of service). Some potential clients might seek help through religion, a hypnotist, or by trying a fad diet that is reputed to stop cravings. These are indirect competitors outside the umbrella of traditional drug and alcohol services. Finally, the rehabilitation center might note statistics that indicate that most individuals with addiction problems do not seek help at all, especially during the earlier stages of the problem. They are choosing inactivity.

In order to thoroughly identify and study competitors, the rehab center must look at all the alternatives available to a person with a drug and alcohol problem. The rehabilitation center may choose to expand its services to offer other types of drug and alcohol services and therefore enter into direct competition with other providers in those areas. In any case, its marketing task is to be more attractive than any of the other alternatives available.

The issue of competition can be quite complex. Although a manufacturer of laundry detergent can be relatively sure that most of us are using one of a limited number of brands, a nonprofit that seeks to identify, profile, and analyze its competitors may need to conduct market research studies simply to determine who they are.

COMPETITION FOR RESOURCES

Thinking about competitors in the nonprofit arena does not sound very nice. Nonprofits, after all, are supposed to be humanistic, mission-driven, do-gooder organizations that work together in the best interest of those in need. Oh, for an ideal society in which this could be true! In fact, nonprofits compete with one another for many resources, and the competition in many cases is as real and intense as one would find in a hard-nosed, for-profit business. It is in the best interest of the organization and those it serves to be aware of the factor of competition in its marketplace. There are many resources for which nonprofits compete, and we will examine a few.

Funding

There is limited funding available in areas such as mental health, education, the arts, and social services, with many agencies competing for a piece of the pie. As if that reality were not ugly enough, there also is a great deal of competition among nonprofits for the dollar, for example:

• When the individual donor reaches the mailbox, weary from a day's work, that potentially generous individual may face appeals from several disease organizations, arts groups, and organizations that propose to rescue children, foreign and domestic, from a variety of ills. All may seem like worthy causes, but the potential donor has limited funds and a healthy dose of skepticism. By the time the checks are written, the charitable dollar is allocated among a few fortunate organizations, if it is forthcoming at all.

• Corporations and foundations review proposals from a variety of organizations, some of which would not be thought of as direct competitors for clients or customers. Yet they must allocate their charitable gifts among the organizations they deem to be worthiest.

• The government allocation process, imperfect though it is, makes funding decisions regarding many different causes and organizations. Unfortunately, the causes that we see as having the greatest needs are not always those that receive the greatest financial support because of political pressures and other factors.

This issue constitutes one of the major challenges facing nonprofit organizations today—working to market the organization effectively to those who control the purse strings. In order to do this, the organization must prove to be more appealing than others who seek the same funds.

Volunteers

Many nonprofit organizations would cease to exist if they could not depend on a volunteer workforce. Because of changing demographics and social structures, however, there is a diminishing pool of potential volunteers. Mom now is in the corporate boardroom, and Granny is off on a tour with the senior citizens' group. The middle-class homemaker and the idle elderly, long the traditional volunteers, may be vanishing breeds. Nonprofits face considerable competition in recruitment and retention of volunteers.

Many organizations are in need of voluntary contributions of time to work with clients or patients, stuff envelopes, answer telephones, or provide a number of needed services. Developing a strategy for reaching out to potential volunteers, bringing them into the organization, and ensuring their satisfaction with the volunteer experience becomes a crucial marketing task as well.

Clients or Customers

In the nonprofit sector, some organizations have waiting lists of would-be consumers who in a sense are competing for the resources of the organization. But many organizations compete for clients or customers, which is the type of competition most commonly found in for-profit corporations.

There are many types of organizations that compete for consumers, including nursing homes, hospitals, daycare centers, counseling centers, and churches. In these cases, the organization is competing with other similar organizations, and their ability to attract consumers will be a vital ingredient in their survival. Other organizations, such as disaster relief organizations, food banks, and sheltered workshops for the retarded tend not to compete for clients—as a matter of fact, they may have more potential clients than their capacity to serve. Their marketing tasks might emphasize the competition for other resources such as funding and volunteers.

Publicity or Visibility

Due to limited promotional budgets, nonprofit organizations are always seeking positive publicity. Not only is it free, but publicity can prove more valuable than paid promotion because it may be better noticed and perceived as credible. However, the local media can only deal with a limited number of press releases and feature stories about the good works of nonprofit organizations.

Nonprofits compete for the inside track with the media and for the honor of having the splashiest or most unique event that will warrant media attention. This type of visibility is vital to fund raising and the competition for other resources. A nonprofit that manages to put itself in the news will have an easier time competing in many arenas, armed with a scrapbook of press clippings and a positive public image.

Board Members

Board members are a resource worth competing for. No organization seeks a board composed of lazy, idle poor people with nothing much to do. It is those willing to contribute work, wealth, and wisdom who are in demand as board members. And they are in demand by many organizations.

Although it may not be unusual to find the names of local corporate CEOs or old money philanthropists on the stationery of many nonprofit organizations, the competition for board members who will make a contribution is significant. Many wise organizations develop a board recruitment plan to ensure good board members and groom effective leaders for the future. This is clearly a marketing plan in itself, in that the organization is seeking and competing for a scarce resource—board members who will provide and/or obtain financial support for the organization while providing expertise and governance. Movers and shakers in the community may be asked to be on the boards of several organizations. Each organization needs a strategy to make itself an attractive organization in order to recruit and retain the leaders of the future.

ANALYZING COMPETITORS

Identifying with whom the organization competes for resources can be a difficult and painful exercise. However, the next step in looking at the marketplace is to analyze each competitor.

Gaining information on competitors may be easy or difficult, depending upon the type of information sought. Sometimes a wealth of information about revenue, programs, and plans can be contained in an annual report, available to the public. Similarly, maintaining files of press clippings on their activities can be helpful. Often, staff members have access to the inside scoop through membership in the same professional organizations or knowing their staff or clients. The Freedom of Information Act allows the public access to financial information regarding nonprofit organizations. It may be a simple task to put together a preliminary profile of competitors without any major digging.

Some nonprofits have entered the cutthroat arena of competitive analysis. They will send a staff member or consultant posing as a potential client to get a tour and answers to many questions. They will place phone calls or request materials under false pretenses. They will count cars in a competitor's parking lot to estimate the volume of their services. Although a far cry from the original mission and vision of nonprofit helpfulness, these and other techniques represent the nature of competition in the nonprofit world today.

Earlier, we discussed the SWOT analysis—the examination of the strengths, weaknesses, opportunities, and threats of the organization. A similar exercise can be useful when conducting a competitive analysis. By examining the internal strengths and weaknesses of the competition, it is possible to identify some areas in which competition is likely to succeed and others in which the competitor simply is too strong and formidable to tackle. A competitor's strength also may indicate a growing market that may be able to support a new, competing program by a second organization. Looking at the opportunities and threats faced by competitors will give the organization some clue regarding the competitor's future, and what its strategy might be.

It can be helpful to list significant competitors, along with what resources they are competing for. They can be classified as major or minor competitors, with attention focused on analyzing and strategizing in cases where competition is deemed to be significant.

COOPERATION VS. COMPETITION

Perhaps the ideal situation from the standpoint of serving the client and cutting organizational one-upsmanship is one in which two or more organizations band together and offer complementary rather than competing products and services. In some cases, mergers have even occurred when two organizations realized that they essentially were duplicating one another's missions and that no one, including the competing organizations, was benefiting from the situation.

Funders tend to frown on duplication of services and ask how the organization proposes to offer something that is not a clone of other organizations' programs. In many cases working with another organization on a cooperative project can appeal to potential funding sources as well.

In some cases, a competitor is too formidable to tackle, and the wisest move may be to concede the market, accepting the fact that a fledgling effort to enter the ring is doomed to failure against a well-established and reputable program. It also may be in the best interests of the client to offer needed programs not available elsewhere and to work with similar organizations to develop a referral network representing a continuum of services that are aimed at the client rather than organization needs.

USING INTERNAL AND EXTERNAL ANALYSES: THE ORGANIZATION'S STRATEGIC POSITION

Although the pursuit of information can be challenging and exhilarating, it should never be a goal in itself. Developing comprehensive profiles of the internal and external environments is a tool in the development of an organizational marketing strategy. Let's flash back to the marketing definition presented in chapter one.

Marketing is:

- A means of identifying what is wanted and needed
- A mechanism for bringing an individual or group that has wants or needs together with an individual or group that can satisfy those wants or needs
- A focus on understanding and serving the client, customer, or consumer

The analyses discussed in this chapter should be geared to assisting in fundamental marketing tasks. If done well, there are some very clear connections.

Both internal and external analyses will yield useful data on what is wanted and needed. By analyzing client profiles, competitors' offerings, and the realities of the external environment, the organization can make some educated guesses regarding the wants and needs of its target groups. Environmental scanning of social, economic, and other factors will provide insight into the current and future needs and wants the organization might serve. Internal data also will provide valuable information regarding past wants and needs of those served by the organization and will allow a basis for projecting into the future.

The marketing function of bringing those with wants and needs together with those who can be of service is made infinitely easier if the organization pinpoints those wants and needs and identifies where the services are most needed. This activity depends on the availability of solid information concerning the wants and needs of those to be served, as well as how they might best be reached. The types of conclusions drawn from internal and external analyses will assist the organization in bringing their offerings to an interested public.

Satisfying consumer needs also is easier when the organization develops a solid understanding of who its consumers are, what competitors stand ready to meet unsatisfied wants and needs, and how the needs of those consumers are likely to change in the future. By analyzing internal data such as client profiles and external data such as social and economic trends, the organization can gain an accurate perception of how it can best fulfill its mission.

These elements are important in marketing strategy. In order to plan for a marketable organization, managers must have the best available information at their disposal, which allows informed decisions to be made regarding the future.

REVIEW QUESTIONS

1. What are primary and secondary data and what are some advantages and disadvantages of each?
2. What is meant by the terms internal and external data? Give several examples of each.
3. What is an internal analysis and why is it important to the organization?
4. What is meant by environmental scanning?
5. List some of the major environmental factors that nonprofits might track and give several examples of each.

6. Are zoos, organizations for underprivileged children, and retirement communities competitors? Explain your answer.

7. What are some of the resources for which nonprofits typically compete?

8. What might be some advantages of deciding to cooperate or concede the market rather than compete?

9. What is the relationship between internal and external analysis and marketing strategy?

10. How does information analysis help the nonprofit fulfill its mission?

MINI CASE STUDY

Old Friends is a senior service organization whose mission is to serve the social and recreational needs of the community's residents over sixty years of age. It receives funding from several sources, governmental and private. In the five years since Old Friends was established, it has grown from a small program to a large, multifaceted program. Now it has opened a second location in an adjoining area, six blocks from the bus line.

Jane Spencer, the director of Old Friends, is concerned that the attendance at some of the programs has dropped off in the past year. Activities such as crafts classes and chair exercise are poorly attended, and the organization has experienced some dissatisfaction among its clients who grumble that the activities offered are "boring" and "the same old thing." The director has noticed that younger people (ages sixty to sixty-five) are attending a few times, then not returning. She also has seen that some of her most loyal clients are over age seventy-five.

Jane is concerned about the organization's future. Based on what she sees and hears, she believes that the organization needs some new life and new programs but is unsure of what the clients want and will utilize. At this point, she is afraid to do anything for fear of wasting scarce resources on an unsuccessful offering. The second location has been poorly utilized since it opened, and the things that are popular at the first site are not popular there. Jane doesn't understand how older people who live just down the road could be any different.

Jane contemplates what to do to avoid the organization's becoming irrelevant and dying a slow death. She knows that there are changes occurring over which she has no control but doesn't know how to pinpoint them.

1. How might the concepts of internal and external analysis be helpful to Jane Spencer?

2. What factors in environmental scanning might be most important in looking at the future of Old Friends?

3. What type of demographic analysis might be beneficial in this case?
4. What types of internal and external data would you recommend Jane collect on a routine basis to give her a better handle on her problems?

FURTHER READING

Espy, Siri N. Are You in Step With Your Community's Needs? *Nonprofit World*, 7(2), March/April 1989, 28–29.

———. *Handbook of Strategic Planning for Nonprofit Organizations*. New York: Praeger Publishers, 1986.

Johnson, Eugene M. Situation Analysis for Nonprofit Marketing Planning. *Nonprofit World*, 4(4), July/August 1986, 26–29.

Kotler, Philip. *Marketing for Nonprofit Organizations*. Englewood Cliffs, NJ: Prentice Hall, 1982.

———. *Principles of Marketing*. Englewood Cliffs, NJ: Prentice Hall, 1986.

CHAPTER 5

Knowing Your Market: Marketing Research in the Nonprofit

Attendance at the Single Again Center is down. There has been a lack of interest in the activities and support groups at the center, and several long-standing programs are in danger of cancellation. The staff members of the organization hold a special meeting to talk about the future of their services. Although there are many theories among those present, no one has any answers. In frustration, the executive director asks, "What do these people want?"

Marketing research helps managers to answer precisely this question—what do people want and need? There are many stakeholder groups the nonprofit must serve and satisfy, and understanding who they are and how to serve them is essential to the fulfillment of the organization's mission.

For-profit corporations and larger nonprofits might make sizable investments in marketing research, employ specialized in-house research departments, or contract with professional research firms to answer questions related to the market for the goods and services offered by the organization. Smaller nonprofits with more severe budgetary constraints often must deal with less extensive and methodologically sound information in their quests for the truth about the market(s) they exist to serve. In any case, an effective organization will work to gather as much data as possible within its limitations.

WHAT IS MARKETING RESEARCH AND WHY IS IT IMPORTANT?

Marketing research can take many forms, but it primarily is a tool for collecting and analyzing market-related data to aid in making decisions regarding marketing and planning issues. Marketing research questions and concerns ideally should be based on the strategic plan, which sets organizational goals and identifies target markets. The research will work toward providing key information about those target groups and identify organizational strengths and weaknesses that affect its ability to reach the identified goals.

Marketing research is a vital means of gathering information and input into the marketing process. Again, we can identify the relationship between this activity and our definition of marketing.

Marketing research aids in understanding wants and needs. As the staff of the Single Again Center has discovered, it is important to understand what the target market wants and needs in order to provide offerings that will be utilized and appreciated. Marketing research can help the organization understand important constituencies and pinpoint their wants and needs.

Many organizations talk about conducting a needs assessment; this simply is a measure of the wants and needs of a particular group of people in a specific area. In fact, an effective needs assessment is a form of market research if we look at marketing and its role in fulfilling the organization's mission and determining wants and needs. Needs assessments give the organization information about what programs and services should be provided— information about the target markets of the organization.

Marketing research helps the organization reach out to potential consumers and other important groups and fulfill mission-related wants and needs. Gathering sound information regarding the wants, needs, attitudes, and preferences of important groups will help the organization to reach out to them. A marketing appeal will be ineffective if it is not tailored to a target audience, and marketing research can help the organization to understand and effectively appeal to those targets.

Marketing research can measure and help ensure continued satisfaction. The marketing task clearly has not been completed when the organization makes contact with or provides service to the consumer. Marketing research assists in identifying areas of satisfaction and dissatisfaction that form important parts of the organization's image and affect its ability to fulfill its mission.

QUESTIONS THAT CAN BE ANSWERED BY MARKETING RESEARCH

Nonprofit organizations are faced with a number of questions related to their mission and markets. They must decide who to serve, in what way, and what activities or programs will be of most interest and assistance to those target groups. Whether the research takes the form of informal interviews or scientifically designed studies, it can assist in a number of ways, a few of which are detailed below.

Determining Wants and Needs

Often the organization attempts to serve one or more target groups by relying on educated guesses regarding their wants and needs. In some cases, this is ineffective, and the organization may choose to ask these target groups to assist by identifying their wants and needs and telling the organization how it can best serve them, for example:

- An organization that supports those with a specific disease asks for input from clients and their families regarding desired services.
- A program for adoptive families surveys clients to determine what needs are unmet.
- An arts program asks local families for ideas on a young people's program.
- A development director tracks response rates from several different types of appeals to determine their effectiveness.
- An employment counseling service interviews local economic development experts.

All these activities are geared toward making decisions concerning program issues based on information from and about those who will be affected by those decisions.

Assessing Attitudes and Reputations

Attitudes are powerful determinants of human behavior. An organization affected by a particular image or community attitude ideally should be aware of these factors and how they can affect efforts to do business, positively or negatively. Likewise, the way people feel about themselves in relationship to the organization will be important in the marketing effort. These intangible but vital considerations might include:

- Residents over sixty-five who are reluctant to become involved with the senior center because "it's for old fuddy-duddies."
- A local health clinic experiences good utilization because of a reputation for caring, quality treatment.
- People experiencing mild adjustment and marital problems avoid the counseling center because they aren't "crazy."
- Performances at the civic art center often are sellouts because the community appreciates the good work done there.
- Lower-income persons are unwilling to go to a community help center because they "pry into your business."

An organization that understands attitudes such as these is better able to capitalize on positive perceptions and work to overcome negative ones. Instead of scratching one's head in puzzlement regarding a poor reception or failing to fully exploit a good one, organizations can attempt to study the attitudes that help to determine that success or failure.

Evaluation of Communication Efforts

Many nonprofits rely on some form of formal organizational communication to get the word out about their good work and to attract resources. This communication can include brochures, letters, public service announcements, advertising, or a speakers' bureau. Research efforts can help the organization to determine reaction to these communication efforts both before and after taking them public, for example:

- An organization determines that its brochure includes professional jargon and terms that are not appropriate for its target audience.
- Very few members of the target audience for a public information campaign had seen the information.
- The idea for a public service announcement really does not capture the agency's strong points.
- The proposed fund-raising letter is too hard hitting and does not emphasize the merit of the activities to be supported.

By evaluating a communication plan before it is implemented, the organization can save valuable resources and avoid negative consequences. Measuring the impact after the campaign can make help the organization to determine its effectiveness and improve the next communication effort.

New Offering Research

Many organizations waste scarce resources by starting a new program or offering without first doing their homework. It is easy to assume that the staff, with their professional training and expertise, will be able to anticipate the market for the organization's new ideas. Unfortunately, that is not always the case. Doing some preliminary research prior to major investments can help the organization to anticipate the success or failure of a new idea.

- An organization that is considering an afterschool program for children discovers that there already are many competing programs with which parents are highly satisfied.
- The planetarium discovers that there is little interest among local school districts in participating in a science project.
- A mental health program gets an enthusiastic response to a proposed recreation program from clients and their families.
- A domestic violence program discovers that there is a need for

additional shelter facilities for women with young children in the community.

By investing a little additional time and energy in researching an idea prior to startup, organizations can be assured that they are channeling their resources toward programs and services that will be well utilized and effective in fulfilling the wants and needs of target groups.

Market Size Analysis

Either prior to startup or when considering issues of expansion and future direction, organizations often need an estimate of how large the potential market for a program or service might be. This information will help the organization determine whether entry or expansion into a particular market is warranted and whether the future is promising for its offerings.

- An organization serving the frail elderly wants to estimate how many individuals will be needing their services in the next five years.
- A religious organization must decide whether it will need to expand its physical facilities to meet increased demand.
- A retirement community tries to determine how many affluent retirees will be interested in and able to afford its housing.
- The hospice wants to determine whether there is a need for its services in neighboring communities.

Questions such as these require information about the size of the market. There is often no point in expanding services in a saturated market, where a high level of satisfaction exists with plentiful competing programs. However, if there are unmet needs, the organization will want to know and be prepared to react. Organizations also need to plan ahead. If a new facility, additional staff, or a new program will be needed to meet increased demand, it is important to have this information. Likewise, a program may need to prepare to scale down or change its direction if the market for its present offerings is likely to shrink.

Market Share Analysis

Although for-profit corporations have long tracked their market share, this concept is helpful in determining the position of a nonprofit organization in the group(s) it seeks to serve. Market share simply refers to that portion of the target group an organization serves as opposed to other organizations. For example, if one hundred handicapped individuals in the community require transportation services and your organization serves twenty-five, then you have a 25 percent market share. If extensive information were available, you would be able to determine how the other 75 percent are served, which can give you clues in expanding your market if that is your goal. Market share information can help answer a number of questions, such as:

- Effectiveness in reaching the members of target market(s)
- Growth or decline in market share (if several years' data is available)
- Who else is successfully serving the market (if data on other organizations is available)
- Whether the organization is a major or minor player in the program or service area

In some cases, funders, government agencies, or the organizations themselves may publish statistics regarding the number of persons served in a certain category, thus making a particular organization's share easy to determine. In other cases, a best guess approach may be needed.

Evaluation of Existing Offerings

Often, an organization is unable to pinpoint why its offerings succeed or fail and needs more information to evaluate its existing programs and services. In cases such as these, it is important to have good information about the market and the organization's position in it.

- Is the new location of the support group a factor in the drop in attendance?
- How do people perceive the staff? Are they a plus or a minus in drawing and retaining consumers?
- Are participants pleased with the parenting education program?
- Does our existing day program for retarded adults adequately meet their needs?
- Is our job training program adequately preparing clients to enter the workforce?

Answers to questions such as these can help an organization determine how well it is fulfilling its mission and what factors may be pluses and minuses in these efforts. Without such information, efforts may be well meaning but poorly focused, and the organization can stumble along providing service that is perceived as inadequate or the wrong kind for satisfying existing wants and needs.

Marketing Research in Fund Raising

Fund raising is an activity that depends on the ability to reach potential donors, including individuals, corporations, and foundations. The organization that undertakes an effort to raise funds will need as much information as possible related to the actual or potential success of the campaign. Ineffective fund raising not only costs dollars, it results in lost opportunities and potential alienation of future donors. As a result, nonprofits might seek information such as:

- How are we perceived by potential donors?
- What types of programs is this foundation or corporation interested in funding?
- What motivates people to give to us?
- What factors make us unattractive to potential philanthropists?
- What impression does our fund-raising appeal make?

An organization that understands the attitudes, outlooks, and motivations of its donors is in a better position to effectively launch its appeal. Identifying strengths on which to build and weaknesses to overcome will help the organization increase its donor base.

WHAT DO YOU WANT TO KNOW?

Before an organization can determine answers, it must first come up with the questions. As with any management tool, market research can be used ineffectively, yielding inaccurate and misleading information if the organization does not fully grasp the questions it is attempting to ask. Therefore, it is important to state the problem or question clearly and to anticipate the type of information to be yielded by the project.

- A study to determine client satisfaction may not explain a drop in utilization if family members are frequently the actual decision makers.
- A questionnaire pinpointing clients' difficulty with transportation to the office will not help the organization determine whether other significant problems are sending clients away.
- Market share data will not explain why a jump or drop in a figure occurred.

In designing and carrying out a marketing research project, the organization must be able to determine what it does and does not want to know and to look at its priorities . Even if it were possible to research everything about everybody, the cost and confusion would be staggering. Ideally, research should be broad enough to fully answer the question(s) at hand and even allow for serendipitous findings.

For many organizations, the starting point is determining what it needs to know in order to conduct business. Because of the limited resources with which many nonprofits contend, it is important to look at what information is vital to decisionmaking and what merely is nice to know. Depending on the organization's capabilities, those responsible for the project can determine the size and scope of the project.

How much marketing research is needed is a question that must be answered by each organization. In many cases, the organization has not obtained any market information in the past and will need to make a small and modest start in gathering data. In other cases, organizations may feel that the collection of large amounts of data is a worthwhile investment. The organization always should weigh the costs against the benefits of collecting information, factoring in the risk of acting impulsively without information to back up a decision. Managers must always consider the consequences of making an uninformed decision. The cost savings of abandoning a research effort will be offset by the much greater costs of ignoring the realities of the marketplace. However, the organization may determine that the cost is too high, and will need to settle for little or no information.

PRIMARY VS. SECONDARY RESEARCH

Just as marketing research can serve a number of functions, it also can take many forms. An organization that seeks additional information can rely on a number of types of research.

As with other types of data, marketing research can be primary or secondary. Primary research is carried out by or for a specific organization to address a particular question or problem. Secondary research is conducted by another organization for a different purpose but can be accessed for use. Primary research ideally is custom designed and will be conducted according to the organization's specifications and needs; however, it can be an expensive and time-consuming proposition. Secondary research is readily available in the library or professional publications and can give information on national trends or another market in which the research was conducted. The organization may find such secondary data less useful and too general for its unique situation.

TYPES OF MARKET-RELATED STUDIES

Demographic Research

Demographic data, as we discussed earlier, are a vital part of understanding the environment in which the organization operates. Demographic research frequently is secondary in nature, with government or corporate bodies gathering and sharing data that can be applied to the service area. Demographic research can help answer a number of questions.

- Is the population of this area in need of economic assistance?
- How many elderly residents are currently in our service area, and what is projected for the future?
- What communities in a fifty-mile radius of our office have a high ratio of children?
- Where is population growth expected to occur?

Demographic research always is a good point at which to start, but it should not be used as the final word in making program or service decisions. There are a number of other variables that are important as well. For example, a community with a large number of children may not be an ideal target for daycare if a number of providers already serve the area or if the area is a prosperous one in which stay-at-home mothers or nannies prevail. Demographics give us a rough picture of the service area and may help form further questions on which to focus.

Service Area Profiles

Some organizations work with local government and other sources to develop a comprehensive profile of the geographic area(s) served. This type of analysis can include data concerning expected growth, building permits issued, demographic data, and business and commercial development. Often, local officials will work with the organization to help fill in the gaps in knowledge of the area and share inside information about what is expected to happen in the future. Developing a community profile can provide information, such as:

- Where is residential growth expected?
- Is this area likely to change in terms of population, socioeconomic makeup, or character?
- Are new businesses moving into the area? How many and what kind?

- Are the needs of the area likely to change over the next few years?

An organization planning for the future is better served by having solid information regarding the needs of the area served. In some cases, areas undergo radical changes due to economic problems, progress, new building initiatives, or attraction of major industry to the community. Keeping abreast of such developments will allow the nonprofit to anticipate and plan for changing needs.

Consumer Satisfaction Data

Many organizations that are devoted to serving the needs of a particular group will benefit from systematically collecting and analyzing data regarding satisfaction with the organization's efforts. Surveying or questioning consumers can help answer a number of important questions such as:

- How do our consumers feel about our organization and its offerings?
- What do they feel we do particularly well?
- What do our consumers perceive as our major weaknesses?
- What wants or needs remain unmet in the eyes of our consumers?
- What changes should we make in order to provide better service for our constituents?

Consumer satisfaction data can be difficult to collect; consumers may be unable or unwilling to share their perceptions and getting a significant response can be difficult. In the case of persons with emotional problems or young children, for example, reliable information may not be forthcoming, and the families of clients may be able to provide useful feedback. In any case, it is important for the organization to appreciate that those it exists to serve should have a role in assessing its success and in planning for the organization's future.

Informal Observation—MBWA

Although some might argue that informal observation technically is not research, it is important to consider that without any additional expenditure organizations can have access to many valuable pieces of information. Many managers are proponents of MBWA—Management by Wandering Around. This approach can serve nonprofits on a tight budget. By merely observing and tracking what is happening in the organization, the nonprofit can gather a wealth of information. For example:

- Attendance at activities is heavier on some days than others.
- The average age of clients appears to be rising.
- The members of the professional society have seemed bored by the last several speakers.
- The operator has not received many calls about the new program.

Such information, although not conclusive or scientifically valid, can give the organization valuable insights without large outlays of cash or personnel time. It can suggest trends worth monitoring and can pinpoint areas where additional research is needed. This approach is probably more common in smaller organizations where staff and board members are closer to the action, but it also is important in larger organizations where key leadership easily can be out of touch with the day-to-day happenings that affect the overall marketability of the organization.

Systematic Observation

An organization may observe what goes on and how their constituents react to what is offered. This can be carried out in a number of ways:

- A volunteer counts the number of attendees at the gate of a free event to measure interest in the topic.
- People are stationed at a number of zoo exhibits to count how many people view them to determine their popularity.
- A tally is kept of how many purchases are made by children at the souvenir shop to determine which customers to target.
- An organization sponsoring an information booth tracks the number of men and women who stop and their approximate ages to measure the level of interest in the cause among various groups.

This type of study can give the organization some basic information on the characteristics of its consumers and what appears to interest them, although it leaves unanswered questions regarding their motivations or specific reactions.

Experimental and Quasi-Experimental Methods

Some organizations conduct research that is somewhat experimental in nature, delving into the choices people make and the reasons they are made. Examples of research that falls into this category include:

- Asking participants to choose pictures of people or items they prefer and explain their preference
- Distributing play money and requesting that participants allocate it to available choices according to their wishes
- Eliciting information regarding attitudes by asking respondents to describe what type of people would use the services of the agency

Often, research of this nature allows the organization to approach issues indirectly and may encourage respondents to share their reactions honestly. For example, a senior center may learn that local residents are reluctant to participate in programs because of a perception that it serves "old people" and a job counseling service is losing upscale clients due to an image of serving the hard-core unemployed. In conducting studies that utilize experimental methods, however, research skills are important in designing and developing meaningful projects.

Focus Groups

A focus group is an excellent tool for eliciting feelings and reactions. This technique involves a group of people who are invited to participate in a discussion focused on a specific topic or group of topics. A facilitator guides the discussion, encouraging participants to share their reactions and asking follow-up questions when appropriate. Focus groups can help provide information such as:

- How clients feel about an organization
- The needs of a specific target market
- Why participants would or would not use a particular product or service
- How a service can be made more user-friendly

Focus groups can provide a wealth of information. However, a number of cautions are in order. A skilled facilitator is needed to keep the group on track and ask meaningful questions, and the participants selected must represent those with the opinions that matter most. Summarizing and interpreting findings is subjective and imprecise, and subject to the bias of the facilitator. Focus groups often are videotaped to allow for viewing by a number of individuals within the organization. A focus group can serve as a preliminary tool for identifying which questions or issues to pursue in a formal market research endeavor.

Survey Research

Many organizations conduct surveys at some point to gather information regarding the external environment, internal operating factors, or the constituents it exists to serve. Surveys can help in a number of ways:

- Assessing employee satisfaction
- Determining needs as perceived by other agencies
- Soliciting input from actual or potential consumers
- Measuring attitudes toward an organization or issue

Surveys typically contain several types of questions:

- **Closed-ended questions** include true-false, multiple choice, and rating scale items that force the respondent to choose among responses included on the survey form. Such questions are clear and unambiguous and force the respondent to choose from a manageable number of alternatives. Results are therefore easy to tabulate. However, there are disadvantages as well. A closed-ended question does not allow for any explanation of the answer; whether the implication of the answer is negative or positive, the question does not provide for feedback on peripheral issues or encourage "accidental" findings due to their rigid structure.

Examples:

- How would you rate the cleanliness of our facility?
  a. Good   b. Fair   c. Poor
- Who referred you to this program?
  a. Friend
  b. Family
  c. Clergy
  d. Other _____

- **Open-ended questions** ask for reactions or comments on a specific issue. They allow for a full explanation of the answer and can provide a great deal of depth and serendipitous findings. However, the quality of the answers can vary depending on the ability and willingness of the respondent to express thoughts and feelings in writing; many people offer one word or yes/no answers instead of elaborating on the matter at hand or even leave the item blank. It also is difficult and time-consuming to summarize the responses, especially when working with a large number of responses.

Examples:

- How might we improve our services to better meet your needs?

- Please comment on the quality and helpfulness of our staff.

Often, a combination of the two types of questions proves to be most effective and efficient. Providing a number of closed-ended, standard questions that will elicit easily tabulated and interpreted results along with the opportunity to expand on answers and offer comments in an open-ended format will allow for good coverage of the topic(s) in question.

There are several major types of surveys:

Mail questionnaires

Many organizations conduct surveys by mailing questionnaires to a group of preselected people. Mail surveys have specific advantages: they typically are fairly inexpensive to conduct, and they assure uniformity of presentation because all those who respond are asked the same question in the same way. The ability to offer anonymous or impersonal responses by mail may encourage honesty. However, mail surveys often have a low response rate, and respondents may not take the time to answer carefully.

Personal interviews

Talking one-on-one, face-to-face can yield a great deal of interesting information. A skillful interviewer will be able to elicit reactions and more fully understand the sentiments of the interviewee. However, it is time consuming to schedule and devote adequate attention to each individual interview. People may be reluctant to give candid, complete answers, especially regarding negative reactions or information they consider personal or embarrassing in nature. The characteristics of the interviewer also will play a part—imagine a nun conducting a survey on attitudes toward abortion or a member of a racial minority questioning whites regarding integration. Summarizing results can be challenging because of the variety and diversity of responses.

Telephone interviews

Conducting interviews by telephone can combine the best and the worst of mail and personal interview techniques. Telephone conversations provide the advantages and disadvantages of relative anonymity, as the respondent is not face-to-face with the interviewer. However, many people view such inquiries as unwelcome intrusions and refuse to participate. In these days of answering machines and busy dual-career families, the surveyors may have difficulty in finding anyone home to answer!

Sampling is another important issue in conducting surveys. To be scientifically valid, **random sampling** must be used, and the survey must be designed in such a way that the sample size is large enough to assure that it represents the population under consideration. Many nonprofits with limited research budgets use some variation of **convenience sampling**, which provides for surveying those who can be easily reached—such as people who pass by on a certain day or those who attend a specific event. Although this is, as implied, convenient, great caution must be taken in interpreting and generalizing the results. For example, if a survey is conducted on Tuesday in the mental health center and that is the day when the depression support group is held, this may greatly skew the results. Some organizations elect to periodically survey all their consumers, which is most feasible for organizations such as schools, healthcare facilities, daycare centers, and membership organizations with constituencies for which names and addresses are easily accessible. Universal sampling would not be an option in "public" organizations such as a zoo or an art gallery where the visitors are sporadic and records are not kept of their involvement.

USING MARKETING RESEARCH

The effective use of marketing research and information depends upon the ability to analyze and report such data. Although we will not delve into the technical aspects of marketing research, a few considerations are worth mentioning.

Effective summarization of data is vital. Few managers and staffers will be interested in the amount of detail contained in scores of individual responses, and the ability to report aggregate results without losing too much of the "flavor" is an art in itself. Achieving the balance between overload and losing important information requires a knowledge of the organization, its markets, and the information at hand.

Report preparation likewise is a vital part of the undertaking and always should be geared to the audience the report will reach. Often, effective reports are simple in nature, containing an appropriate blend of data tables, charts, graphs, and narrative. If the audience for the report is numbers oriented, a different approach may be needed than one which is best for a qualitatively oriented group. Again, the report should attempt to tell readers what they need to know without bogging them down in detail that obscures the important "big picture."

Once gathered, market-related data should be used. This may be stating the obvious, but all too frequently organizations gather and report data and then proceed to make decisions as though the data did not exist. An organization should not make monumental decisions based on one set of data; the collective data should provide clues as to viable future directions for the organization.

Each individual organization must determine which type of research is needed, ranging from a sophisticated computerized modeling package to a twice-per-year pencil and paper survey and some information in a file drawer. Balancing costs and benefits will yield some idea of the types of information needed to help the organization in decision making and in understanding what the future may hold. It is important, in any case, that the system be maintained and updated periodically as the organization and the world around it change.

ENSURING THE VALIDITY OF MARKETING RESEARCH

Although the benefits of marketing research are considerable, there are a number of limitations that should be considered when interpreting and using the data. It is to the organization's advantage to pay attention to matters of design. Ideally, research should be methodologically sound in that it uses scientific sampling techniques and is interpreted by a trained researcher. However, on a practical level many organizations that need information are constrained by a very limited budget.

In attempting to interpret information, the organization must keep in mind its inherent limitations. At times, the characteristics of those who do not respond are different from those who do. For example, only those who are very satisfied or very dissatisfied with an organization's programs and services may be motivated to respond to a questionnaire, giving a skewed response and allowing for easy misinterpretation of the data. Respondents also may be dishonest or evasive, especially if they feel that their answers will be used in a manner that is not to their benefit. There are a number of reasons why research findings should always be taken with the proverbial grain of salt.

Predicting the future is an art that unfortunately has not been perfected. Even if comprehensive, accurate data exist on past performance (a highly unlikely state of affairs), this information will not necessarily predict future behavior. The world is a busy place and some intervening variable can appear out of the blue and invalidate many years of data. Abrupt changes in demographics, culture, or the characteristics of the nonprofit consumer can render past research findings useless and send the organization scrambling for new information on which to base future decisions.

Research findings also may be used for political purposes. Unfortunately, there is some truth to the saying that figures may not lie but liars can figure; it is possible to design, carry out, and interpret a data-gathering expedition in such a way that it is biased and likely to support a desired conclusion. Maintaining objectivity always is an important issue in research and should be a main concern when a marketing information program is developed.

REVIEW QUESTIONS

1. What is marketing research?
2. How can marketing research help an organization assess issues related to attitude and reputation of the organization?
3. What is market share and why is it important to the organization?
4. What is the difference between primary and secondary marketing research?
5. Why are customer satisfaction data important?
6. What is the difference between informal and systematic observation?
7. What are focus groups and how are they used?
8. What are open-ended and closed-ended questions?
9. What are the major types of surveys, and what are the advantages and disadvantages of each?
10. What are nonresponse errors, and how can they affect the validity of survey findings?

MINI CASE STUDY

Community Living Associates is an organization that provides supportive housing to individuals with mental illness or retardation. It offers supervised living in homes in a community setting for those with a higher degree of impairment and also provides apartments and roommates for individuals able to function on their own.

The organization has several new board members who have an interest in marketing research and feel that it is important to gather and use such data in planning. Initially, the staff is stumped. They had never thought of market research as necessary for them, as they frequently have a waiting list even though they do not advertise their services to the public. In addition, the characteristics of the people they serve make thoughts of marketing research quite foreign. Nevertheless, the board has asked the director to make a report on the type of marketing research and information program the organization might adopt.

1. How might the concepts of marketing research be helpful to Community Living Associates?
2. Which important groups might be the subjects of research?
3. How might the organization best research the needs and satisfaction of this special client population?
4. What might be the role of marketing research in an organization such as this one where attracting additional consumers is not an issue?

5. What resources might this organization be interested in attracting? How could market research help?

FURTHER READING

Dickson, John P. and Sarah S. Dickson. The Importance of Marketing Research to the Nonprofit Organization. *The Nonprofit World Report,* 2(6), November/December 1984, 12–14.

Skloot, Edward. Market Research: Useful Tips, Key Questions. *Nonprofit World,* 6(2), March/April 1988, 8–9.

CHAPTER 6

Products and Services: The Market-driven Organization

Late one night the executive director of Human Service Centers, Inc., is reviewing the last draft of the organization's proposal to provide employee assistance services to a local corporation. She stops and thinks of the old days when the centers only offered counseling services to individuals and families and she reflects on how far the organization has come. Its daycare centers, preschools, and singles programs are relatively recent additions and are all in the black. The organization's contracts with local businesses are successful, and plans to provide adult daycare for the elderly dependents of the corporations' employees are proceeding well. Human Service Centers, Inc., has come a long way, indeed.

In today's world, organizations like this one are proliferating. Faced with declining funding, new social trends, and changing demographics, the entrepreneurial spirit is alive and well in nonprofit organizations. Organizations are realizing that survival into the twenty-first century will require an ability to adapt and change in order to avoid extinction in a climate of rapid evolution.

Nonprofit entrepreneurship is not a contradiction in terms. As noted in chapter one, nonprofits are barred by law from engaging in private inurement—allowing financial successes to benefit individuals in the form of a distribution of profits. However, nonprofits are not prohibited from generating an excess of revenue over expenses, unless specifically stated in a contract or arrangement with a funding or regulating body. Although it might still be unusual to hear one's church discussing profit margins, many nonprofits are recognizing the need to be responsive to the marketplace and fiscally responsible and are seeking new opportunities as a result.

THE PROACTIVE ORGANIZATION

Nonprofit organizations vary in their approach to change. Some organizations offer the program du jour, hopping on every trend and bandwagon, often without adequate planning and with little thought for the future. Others could have as a motto, "Where yesterday's decisions are made tomorrow." However, it is in the best interest of all nonprofits to continually examine the market in looking at the programs, services, and products it will offer in the future.

What the future holds for nonprofit organizations is, of course, uncertain. The days of good people doing good work as a necessary condition of survival most likely are over. The fierce competition for resources, the adoption of for-profit management attitudes and ideas, and the cutbacks in government and philanthropic funding are easily observed in many areas of the nonprofit sector. For the wise organization and its leadership, these elements add up to the need for an innovative, forward-thinking approach to the management of the nonprofit.

Planning for the future of an organization is not merely assembling the pieces of a jigsaw puzzle. It is more like building with blocks—the raw materials can be assembled in a variety of ways to create vastly different configurations. The entrepreneurial, proactive organization will take the building blocks approach and may even go so far as to actively seek additional blocks to enhance the structure of the organization.

At each point in its development the organization is faced with fundamental choices: shall we stay the same or shall we change? For many organizations staying the same is no longer an option. Maintaining the status quo in changing times will place the organization at the back of a long line of organizations competing for scarce resources. The question, then, becomes how to change—in what direction to move and when.

THE PRODUCT LIFE CYCLE

Products and services, like people, tend to move through well-defined, predictable life cycles. The following stages (illustrated in Figure 6-1) are likely to occur in the life of any offering from any type of organization:

• **Inception**—like pregnancy, this is the preparatory stage in which the embryonic idea is nurtured and developed. Plans are made, the

FIGURE 6-1 The Product Life Cycle

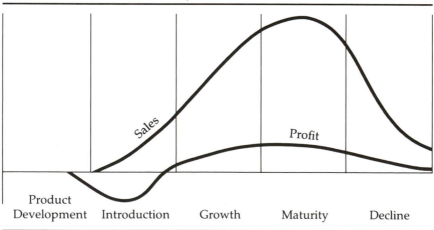

resource requirements are determined and prepared for, and the idea is readied for its introduction to an uncertain future. In this stage, the idea does not contribute in any way to its own support, consuming rather than creating resources.

   • **Introduction**—much as people are born, new ideas are introduced to the cold, cruel world. If the idea is to be a viable one, it will experience at least modest gains within a reasonable time after its introduction. It will begin recouping some of the development costs incurred during the inception stage.

   • **Growth**—any successful offering will experience a period of growth at some point after its introduction to the market. This growth may be slow or rapid.

   • **Maturity**—the newcomer, in time, will mature; slowing or stopping of growth is inevitable in nearly all cases. At this point, funding for the product or service hopefully will be stable.

   • **Decline**—sad to say, nearly all good ideas become outmoded and worn out over time. The organization will be faced with the difficult decision of revising, updating, or eliminating the idea whose time has come and gone.

The entrepreneurial, proactive organization must be aware of these stages and track various programs and services through their life cycles. A look at nonprofit history will yield some ideas that have passed on into the state of decline:

- Foundling homes are obsolete; "desirable" adoptable children are in short supply, and those who are more difficult to place often are cared for in foster homes.
- Tuberculosis hospitals are no longer needed due to the rarity of the disease.
- Homes for "crippled children" have declined with the realization that most of these children can be cared for at home and mainstreamed in school.

On the other hand, there are a number of new ideas that were unheard of several decades ago but are flourishing today, often in the introduction or growth stages:

- Adult daycare for the elderly parents of working families unable to care for them at home
- Ambulatory healthcare and surgery centers
- Deinstitutionalization of people with mental retardation or mental illness

A number of ideas have come and gone in the history of the world, only to make a resurgence. One example is the condom. Sales had declined with the advent of modern methods of birth control, and observers might have predicted that this product was in a final state of decline. However, with the advent of the AIDS crisis, sales of condoms have skyrocketed, with women a new target market as the product is packaged and sold to both sexes.

An organization that is committed to staying in the forefront of its field and offering products and services that are wanted and needed by its target markets will make an effort to keep on top of the life cycle of its offerings. It is not a failure to phase out a program if it has run its course and if new ideas are on the horizon to which scarce resources could better be devoted. In fact, new ideas are healthy and exciting, and an organization whose resources are devoted exclusively to offerings nearing the end of their life cycles could be facing serious difficulty in the near future.

DEVELOPING NEW IDEAS

New ideas are essential to survival. Without them, we would be without all the amenities of modern life, forced to survive in a dismaying world without dishwashers, microwave ovens, and answering machines. Strange to say, even fire and the wheel were once major innovations. An organization that is looking proactively toward its future is always looking for new ideas.

New ideas are everywhere if the organization is open to them:

- Consumers can make valuable suggestions, especially when their input is systematically solicited as discussed earlier.
- Creative board and staff members can have brainstorms that lead to innovative ideas; this can be accomplished through organized brainstorming sessions, in staff meetings, commuting in rush-hour traffic, or in the shower.
- Good ideas can be "stolen" from competitors—what works for one organization can work for another, and reinventing the wheel often is unnecessary.
- Reading professional literature, periodicals, and even the local newspaper can provide the stimulus for new ideas.
- Attending conferences and meetings of professional groups can provide a wealth of new information.
- Board members or other stakeholders can have information about community activities or trends.
- Continued environmental and internal analysis will give the

organization inspiration for changes that can enhance operations.

Some organizations have formal processes for submitting new ideas, and others are more freewheeling in their approach. Whatever the case, the leadership of the organization should create a culture that encourages innovation, stimulating creativity at all levels and pushing the organization to seek new frontiers.

THE PRODUCT–MARKET EXPANSION GRID

Often, one of the easiest and least risky ways for an organization to grow is to build upon current offerings, using skills and resources that already are available, or upon existing markets, taking full advantage of the loyalties of an existing consumer base. The product–market expansion grid (Figure 6-2) can be one tool for examining how that might be possible by generating new ideas.

There are four quadrants within Figure 6-2, each corresponding to a strategy for program/service development.

1. **Market penetration**—an organization opting for the market penetration strategy is concentrating on bringing existing products to existing markets. It is not looking for any new ideas or new types of consumers; its goal is to do more of what it already does:

   • The literacy center looks for more individuals in need of tutoring service.

   • The zoo seeks more visitors to its current facilities and exhibits.

   • A nursing home's goal is to increase its census by admitting more residents to its existing program.

FIGURE 6-2   Product/Market Expansion Grid

	Existing Markets	New Markets
Existing Products	Market Penetration	Market Development
New Products	Product Development	Diversification

This strategy generally carries the smallest short-run risk, because it does not represent any real change in the organization's mission or offerings. In the long-run, however, an organization that sticks with one "product" and one "market" may find itself struggling to exist.

2. **Market development**—this strategy involves bringing existing products to new markets. The goal is to capitalize on knowledge and facilities the organization already has in order to achieve growth. There are several interesting examples of this in the consumer product arena, in both cases driven by socio-demographic changes. When birthrates began falling, manufacturers sought new customers for baby shampoo by appealing to the entire family, and when women entered the workforce in greater numbers and baking "from scratch" declined, the makers of baking soda attempted to convince us that we needed a box in our refrigerators to keep them smelling fresh. Likewise, there are a number of ways nonprofit organizations can work within a market development strategy:

   - A preschool for emotionally disturbed children expands its existing programs to include a class for the educable mentally retarded.

   - A recreation program for active seniors contracts with local nursing homes to provide similar services within their facilities.

   - An AIDS testing and counseling agency that has focused its efforts on the gay community plans for additional outreach to heterosexuals.

In each of these cases, the organization is seeking to do what it does well for a different audience. This strategy represents in most cases slight to moderate short-run risk as the organization is able to change and grow, positioning itself for the future by capitalizing on existing expertise.

3. **Product development**—this strategy is similar to market development above in that it allows the organization to use a current strength as an expansion tool. Product development involves bringing new products into existing markets, so that the organization uses its existing customer base as a focus for expansion of its services:

   - An agency that provides counseling services for victims of domestic violence opens a shelter for these clients.

   - The adoption agency starts a program to provide follow-up counseling to parents tho have adopted special needs children through the agency.

   - A professional society begins offering relevant books and other publications for sale to its membership.

Using the product development strategy is one way that an organization can better fulfill its mission by offering additional products and services to its target group(s). It also is a relatively low-risk option as the organization works with existing consumer groups that presumably it already knows and understands. In addition, the organization's reputation among its consumers as a high-quality provider will facilitate the introduction of a new idea and will provide for growth within an existing market.

4. **Diversification**—an organization seeking to diversify will be bringing new products to new markets. This is clearly the riskiest of the four strategies, because the organization looks for entirely new lines of business. Lessons from the corporate world as well as from nonprofits tell us that the further afield from an established area of expertise the organization ventures, the greater the chance of failure. An organization that does not expand using established skills or markets may find that it lacks the expertise and resources to enter an entirely new arena. Some examples:

   - A hospital purchases a fast-food franchise as a profit-making subsidiary.
   - An organization that successfully operates a retirement community opens a childcare center.
   - An arts center acquires a women's clothing store in a neighboring town.

All of these ventures represent the entrepreneurial spirit at work, yet the organization must take a hard look at whether it has or can reasonably acquire the skills and resources needed for a diversification move, and whether there is a need for involvement in activities that are beyond the scope of its current mission. An organization with little surplus operating capital might do well to stick to other expansion strategies to gain experience before venturing so far outside its proven territory.

The product–market expansion grid is an excellent tool for the nonprofit organization that seeks to grow and change within the boundaries of its mission to provide a specific type of service or to serve a particular target group. This exercise can help the organization identify its options and look at the possibility of using current strengths as springboards for the future.

DEVELOPING CRITERIA FOR EVALUATING NEW VENTURES

An organization that is looking for new opportunities should not move blindly into uncharted territory. Often, it is difficult to determine whether an idea is a good fit with an organization's needs, and a brilliant idea for one organization can be disastrous for another. Developing criteria for evaluating new ventures can help an organization take a hard look at a new idea instead of being swept away in a wave of initial enthusiasm, only to discover later that needed resources were lacking or that the idea did not fit with the organization's mission. The organization can require evaluation of all ideas for new offerings before they are presented for consideration.

Many organizations find it helpful to know in advance what they are fundamentally seeking for the organization. This might be an offshoot of the strategic plan if it has been thoughtfully developed and organizational priorities have been identified. Although each organization must develop its own set of considerations, criteria for new ventures might include items such as:

- **Organizational commitment**—ideally, new programs adopted by the organization should be ones to which the board, staff, and stakeholders are committed. A new venture will stand a better chance at success if the organization feels a sense of excitement and makes a wholehearted commitment to its success.

- **Compatibility with mission**—unless the organization is deliberately seeking to diversify, the potential program should be examined for its fit with the present mission. Perhaps another idea might serve better.

- **Fit with desired image/market position**—an organization that carefully has built an image and position in the marketplace might want to proceed with caution after ascertaining that the proposed new offering will enhance that position. Offering confusing or conflicting messages to consumers can do a great deal of damage to a carefully built image.

- **Size of potential market**—there must be a potential market large enough to justify the addition of any new venture to an organization's set of offerings. An estimated need/want (potential market size) for the new offering will help the organization determine whether the program stands a reasonable chance of success, and whether resources should be allocated.

- **Compatibility with external environment**—factors in the external environment, such as economics, legislative/regulatory factors, and demographics should be examined in order to identify potential roadblocks to the idea's eventual success.

- **Financial considerations**—an organization may need all new ventures to be self-supporting or revenue producing if it is struggling with funding cutbacks or operating losses and is looking for an injection of new funds. An organization that is in the black may be able to subsidize a mission-worthy but unprofitable program.

• **Space availability**—some ideas may require physical space that currently is not available to the organization, and an analysis of the viability and cost of acquiring the space will be needed.

• **Personnel availability**—a new program may necessitate staff additions, possibly involving new types of skills. The availability and cost of additional personnel must be considered.

Although this list certainly is not inclusive, it does suggest that an entrepreneurial organization should not simply take an idea and "run with it," tempting though that approach might be. In order to protect the future while building an adaptive organization, the leadership must explore in depth its resources and their compatibility with new ideas. This process should be an outgrowth of the strategic planning process that sets organizational directions and priorities.

The organization may be able to identify, in advance, specific constraints or priorities that must be considered in connection with all new ideas. For example:

> The Wildwoods Nature Center has discussed its priorities for the next three years as a part of its strategic planning efforts. It has determined that it will look favorably upon proposals that are revenue generating, can use existing facilities, and will enhance visibility and public image in the community.

Given such priorities, this organization can proceed to try to develop new ideas that meet these criteria and discard those that do not. Those that on first examination appear to have sufficient merit to proceed might well be the subject of a feasibility study. However, it is always possible that an idea will come along that has such appeal in other ways that it will overcome an identified weakness and be a smashing success. Flexibility, as always, is the key.

EVALUATING EXISTING PROGRAMS AND SERVICES

Unfortunately, even organizations that conduct detailed feasibility studies on new programs and services often fail to evaluate those already in place. It is important to ask, if we weren't already in this business, would we enter now?

A negative answer does not indicate that a "closed" sign should appear on the door tomorrow, but may be a signal that the program needs to be refined or updated.

Periodically, an organization that seeks to be proactive and innovative should look at all of its offerings. Clearly, there are political consequences to be considered, and an objective evaluation of existing programs is difficult because people often will have a great deal at stake, including their jobs.

Existing programs can be evaluated easily according to criteria such as those proposed above, because there is an operating history of actual facts rather than projections from which to draw. Examination of performance can be conducted, with strengths and weaknesses noted. If the program was created to fill specific needs of the organization or its constituencies, whether human service, financial, or market growth, these factors become evaluation criteria against which to measure the success of the offering. The organization can then make informed decisions regarding the future of that program.

INNOVATION AND RISK

Any organization that avoids a fate of languishing in the status quo must be willing to take a risk. Even the most carefully conducted market study can point in the wrong direction, especially if one or more key factors, such as funding or competitive position, change. The organization must then ask itself how much risk is too much risk.

Nonprofit organizations considering innovative ideas often have a hedge against risk in the form of philanthropy. They can write a grant proposal or solicit donations and seek startup funds for the program, which can greatly diminish the extent to which existing resources are placed at risk for the sake of an unproven idea. If startup costs are covered, the organization need only concern itself, from a financial standpoint, with how soon the program will attain the desired performance in order to avoid draining the organization's resources.

There are, however, many types of risk. Even if a new venture performs well financially, it may pose a drain on other factors, such as image, personnel, space, or stakeholder support. The complex nature of nonprofit organizations and the many groups such as funders, consumers, referrals, and the community affected by them can make decision making and evaluation extremely difficult. At times, a solution that will satisfy one group may alienate another. Using criteria such as those presented above will identify such risks in advance so that strategies for dealing with the downside can be developed.

Clearly, there is no universal formula for determining the optimal level of risk. Innovation always carries with it an element of risk, but often the organization will place itself in greater peril by avoiding new ideas and maintaining the seemingly safe status quo. The organization should consider the potential drain on resources that accompanies all ventures, new and existing, and attempt to prevent placing the soundness of the entire organization in jeopardy over a few poor ideas.

PROFITS FOR NONPROFITS

One strategy that is being adopted by many nonprofits in these changing times is the development of for-profit businesses or subsidiaries to supplement revenues from their nonprofit activities, thus providing a subsidy for programs that may not be self-supporting. If the venture is carefully structured, the organization can realize additional income without jeopardizing the nonprofit, tax-exempt status of the parent organization.

In many cases, the for-profit activities support the nonprofit mission ideologically as well as financially. An organization that promotes education might spawn a publishing business, and a hospital might acquire a durable medical equipment business, offering wheelchairs, crutches, and oxygen to its patients when they are discharged. The nonprofit also might utilize its existing resources in a different manner, such as renting out unused facilities or capitalizing on staff expertise by providing consulting services to other organizations.

Nonprofits must keep careful track of their "business" ventures in the pursuit of additional revenues. While tax laws are in a current state of flux, they merit careful watching as organizations increasingly undertake entrepreneurial ventures. Unrelated business income tax (UBIT) is one issue that nonprofits must track, as excessive "profits" from a venture not directly related to the organization's mission may jeopardize the tax-exemption of the entire organization. If revenues from a venture become substantial, it might be considered for spinoff into a for-profit subsidiary.

Nonprofits, unfortunately, are caught in a difficult bind in considering the role of entrepreneurial, profit-making ventures in ensuring their future survival. Nonprofit organizations increasingly are called upon to be more self-sufficient and find alternate means of support as funding cutbacks occur. Organizations whose leadership take this charge seriously may feel that they have solved or abated their financial problems yet have created another set of equally serious problems:

- For-profit businesses become competitors and may withdraw support from or fight the nonprofit. Many complain that the nonprofit has an unfair advantage due to its ability to use tax-exempt and charitable dollars for venture capital.
- Past donors, including individuals, corporations, and foundations, may perceive that the organization is no longer in need of support and look for "worthier" causes.
- Government funding, based on "need," can be cut if the organization is able to support its expenses through business activities.
- A board and/or staff that provided competent leadership in

the mission-related activities of the organization may lack the skills and vision to compete in the for-profit arena.

• The culture of the organization may not support the demands of a profit-making venture. A nonprofit's altruistic, humanistic focus will not necessarily be at odds with generating revenue, but in some cases a different approach may be needed.

• Resources such as capital, staff, and space can be drawn away from existing programs into the profit-making venture, impairing the organization's ability to carry forth the activities it was founded to perform.

Although some organizations have found that for-profit activities are an enhancement to their revenue base and ultimate survival, the organization should tread carefully into new waters, examining what it hopes to accomplish and studying the feasibility of the new venture. The organization also should be aware of the potential schism created if the mission-related activities ultimately are at odds with the entrepreneurial ventures. When push comes to shove, where does the organization place its priorities and its resources? Prior to startup, the answer may seem clear, but the issue may become problematic if the for-profit venture thrives and the original program languishes. What is important, and how does the organization proceed?

DEVELOPING PARTNERSHIPS: ALLIANCES BETWEEN NONPROFITS AND FOR-PROFITS

Nonprofits increasingly are seeking the company of others as they move toward an uncertain future. They are forming partnerships with for-profit corporations in order to take advantage of the considerable resources brought to the arrangement. Often, such a partnership can provide for optimal use of the resources of both organizations:

• An amusement center offers a specified number of free tokens to those who purchase a token card and advertises that proceeds will go to a local charity. In this case, the business is gaining goodwill and encouraging return visits, while the charity receives increased donations as well as the publicity of having its name associated with a popular attraction.

• A department store features adoptable children as models in a fashion show and provides information on how to adopt. The store gains favorable publicity and shows off its spring line of children's clothing; the adoption agency gets increased visibility, an opportunity to educate the public, and additional calls about adopting the children in the show and others.

- A television station features children who are waiting for foster grandparents or other adult companions. The station gets a public-appeal segment, and the foster grandparent program generates additional interest in volunteering to work with such children.

- A major manufacturer of consumer products donates ten cents to charity for every coupon redeemed. Sales of the products increase, and the nonprofit organization also gets free publicity and additional revenue.

These and similar ventures might be thought of as **cause related marketing,** because the for-profit partner's marketing efforts are related to a specific "good cause." This can be a valued partnership for both organizations, with significant benefits on both sides.

However, as in all ventures, there also is a downside risk. Some industries, such as the tobacco and alcohol industries, increasingly are being shunned as partners in good works because of a general distaste for their products and a growing perception that such businesses are fundamentally damaging to society, especially its vulnerable youth. The nonprofit also can become involved with a corporation whose image somehow becomes tainted by scandal or impropriety during the course of the association and can suffer as a result. A thorough investigation of any potential partner is a necessary first step in what will hopefully become a fruitful working relationship.

Nonprofits seek other types of partnerships with for-profit corporations in the form of contracts and business arrangements:

- A nonprofit organization provides counseling services to the employees of a corporation and their families.

- Educational materials relating to safety issues that are produced by a nonprofit are provided to all newly hired employees at a local manufacturing plant.

- Corporate offices are cleaned by clients of a sheltered workshop that provides work training and job opportunities for individuals with mild mental retardation.

Scenarios such as these represent just a few of the ways nonprofits can serve the needs of their communities as well as work toward their own long-term survival by expanding their markets and seeking new activities.

NONPROFIT PARTNERSHIPS: ORGANIZATIONS WORKING TOGETHER

As nonprofit organizations face difficult times, often they must seek new partners from among nonprofit organizations. Although the nonprofit may seek opportunities to branch out into new arenas, the risk to scarce resources may convince organizations that there is strength in numbers. Nonprofits may seek to develop partnerships in a number of areas:

- Nonprofit hospitals may join together to acquire an expensive piece of equipment, allowing both to remain competitive by having access to the technology but minimizing the risk and financial burden associated with its acquisition.

- Several nonprofits may team together to share facilities or negotiate a more favorable lease by occupying a larger area than either alone would occupy.

- Nonprofits may decide to develop referral agreements, such as an organization for divorced parents that provides support and recreation but refers members to a counseling center rather than duplicate these services.

Although many organizations are reluctant to surrender control and deal with the challenges intrinsic in collaborative efforts, in the future such arrangements certainly are worth consideration. In order to continue to serve the wants and needs of individuals according to the organizational mission, partnerships may be a viable way to survive.

TRADE-OFFS AND SACRIFICES: FACING THE INEVITABLE

In the ideal world, the nonprofit might not be all things to all people, but it would strive to offer a full spectrum of services to its target groups and fulfill its mission through identifying, filling, and following up on client needs. However, in this imperfect world, human needs and worthy causes do not always receive the resources and attention they merit. For this reason, nonprofits may face the unpleasant task of making cutbacks and retrenching in bad times. If efforts fail to market the need to funding bodies, the organization may have no choice but to consider how to cut costs, which may mean cutting valued programs and services. Although no organization relishes this task, the framework of strategic marketing can provide some tools for making some decisions by identifying questions to evaluate where cuts can best be made:

- **Is there some way to provide this program or service at a lower cost?** Upon careful examination, the organization may find that there are ways to streamline operations without making significant changes in the quality or availability of the service. Hospitals, for example, have found that performing preoperative tests on an outpatient basis prior to admission cuts length of stay and therefore, costs without negatively impacting the outcome of the procedure. Similarly, drug and alcohol rehabilitation centers have found that outpatient treatment can be as effective as inpatient rehabilitation at a much lower cost. Some mental health clients may benefit more from group therapy than from individual therapy, with less investment of staff time, or properly trained and supervised volunteers may prove quite effective in working with troubled children. Creative people can develop solutions to resource crunches that do not significantly affect the quality and scope of the organization's offerings.

- **Is this program or service still of major importance to our mission?** Organizations may find that some of their once-valued offerings are no longer of much value or interest and that judicious cutbacks can be made without negative consequences. Programs and services can take on a life of their own, nurtured by those who have invested in them beyond the point of their general usefulness. Periodic evaluation of the organization's programs can help with the weeding-out process, but for many organizations it takes a crisis to precipitate a needed change.

- **Who else offers or duplicates this program or service?** Nonprofit organizations may find that networking or affiliating with other organizations, formally or informally, will help fill service gaps in the face of cutbacks. Two organizations offering similar programs may find that consolidation of services will provide for more efficient, cost-effective programs that have increased survivability. If such a partnership is not feasible or desirable, the organization may choose to cut services that are readily available elsewhere.

- **What are our organizational priorities?** A strategic planning process that is alive and well in an organization will help the organization identify its priority programs and services. If the organization has completed such a plan, the plan should identify the vital programs and initiatives and help provide guidelines for weeding out in times of resource shortage. Priorities might be assigned by examining a number of factors, such as the number of persons served, program costs, fundability, the availability of duplicate services, and the future prospects of the offering, with some numerical weight attached to each factor. Such exercises can help the organization to be as critical and objective as possible when evaluating where cutbacks should occur

- **What can we learn from this dilemma?** As thinking, rational beings, we always should strive to learn from our mistakes. Too often in organizational life, a problem is solved or a crisis averted without sufficient attention to the genesis of the situation. The organization is then doomed to repeat mistakes or to make new ones. If cutbacks are needed, the organization should take a hard look at why they occurred. Blaming the situation on a drop in government funding or charitable giving may be a convenient and even accurate reason, but the wise organization will look beyond the obvious to determine what really went wrong. Perhaps earlier attention to the problem, a better marketing approach, a more timely search for alternate funding, or cost containment might have prevented the crisis. Although hindsight sometimes is considered useless, it can help the organization be effective, efficient, lean, and mean in the years ahead.

MAINTAINING "NONPROFIT" VALUES IN TIMES OF CHANGE

One of the fundamental virtues of nonprofit organizations, as we noted earlier, is that they are not driven exclusively by the profit motive. It is, therefore, a delicate balancing act to become entrepreneurial and proactive without losing the essence of mission and involvement with those groups the organization was founded to serve. In any organization, keeping the mission in mind during times of change is a constant challenge.

Losing the spirit that led to the organization's inception can be a fundamental loss, although a change in mission may be necessary and appropriate if the organization is to evolve and keep up with the world around it. The board and staff members are responsible for keeping what is important in sight. If the organization changes in such a way that it loses the support of its constituencies and key leadership, it suffers a decline in its effectiveness.

DEALING WITH ORGANIZATIONAL CHANGE

Nearly all organizations resist change. Change carries with it implied threats—loss of security, disruption of a comfortable status quo, even possible loss of livelihood if programs are restructured and positions eliminated. Often, the organization that seeks to foster entrepreneurship and adaptation must first look within.

Nonprofits generally were founded on the vision of a person or group of people wanting to "make a difference." This vision often is deep seated and personally meaningful and in many cases leads to the commitment of many hours of volunteer time and hard-earned dollars to a deserving cause. Changing the organization in any way can result in a ripple effect that can lead to human reactions ranging from discomfort to outright revolt.

Those in leadership positions within the organization must realize that such reactions are to be expected and often are the price that must be paid for a committed, altruistic group of staffers, supporters, and stakeholders. A need for change that might be obvious to those who are examining cold, hard data will need to be sold softly over time to those with a stake in doing things "the old way."

Students of organizational behavior have determined that people respond most favorably to change when it is introduced gradually and rationally and when the reasons are carefully explained. Participative management is extremely helpful in garnering the support of key individuals and groups in times of change and also may yield viewpoints and perspectives that will prove beneficial. People need to understand that the change ultimately will protect rather than threaten the future of the organization and that their role is vital to its success. Although managers become impatient with those who impede the forces of change, it is important for them to recognize the loss that comes with giving up the status quo and to work to develop the art of motivating and inspiring those involved with the organization to meet the challenge of the future.

REVIEW QUESTIONS

1. Briefly describe the concept of the product life cycle and the phases that typically are part of this cycle.
2. What are some likely sources of new ideas? How can new ideas be encouraged?
3. What is the product–market expansion grid, and how can it help the nonprofit identify new opportunities?
4. Why does an organization need criteria for evaluating new ideas? What might these criteria include?
5. Why should an organization evaluate its existing offerings?
6. How should an organization work to balance innovation and risk?
7. What are some of the potential negative consequences of engaging in a for-profit activity?
8. How and why are nonprofits forming partnerships with for-profit corporations?
9. How can an organization balance mission with the need for entrepreneurial activity?
10. Why is effective management of organizational change important to the proactive, entrepreneurial organization?

MINI CASE STUDY

The Community Children's Center was founded five years ago as a place where mothers in a medium-sized city could bring their children for a variety of activities. The center has story hour three times a week, a toy lending library, and various activities for children, such as crafts classes and song fests. The center started as a small, grassroots organization founded by a group of mothers concerned because there was nowhere to go to meet other mothers and to provide educational and recreational programs for their children.

Over the past five years, however, the center has been successful beyond the dreams of its founders. Membership and attendance have skyrocketed, fed in large part by the city's economic development and the resulting attraction of many young families to the area. Many of the center's programs have waiting lists, and there is a problem with too much demand for too few resources.

The board is contemplating the future of the center and wondering in which direction to go. There currently is some divisiveness among board members regarding the posture the organization should take. Various options have been mentioned, ranging from limiting membership to levels that could be accommodated by the present programs and facilities to expansion that might include satellite facilities and the startup of new programs, such as a daycare center and preschool to serve the community and corporate sector as they grow.

1. How should the board approach building an entrepreneurial, proactive organization?
2. What are the risks in taking an innovative, growth-oriented position? How might they best be handled?
3. Can you make a case for maintaining the status quo despite pressures for growth and change? What might it be?

FURTHER READING

Caesar, Patricia. Cause-Related Marketing: The New Face of Corporate Philanthropy. *Nonprofit World*, 5(4), July/August 1987, 21–26.

Crimmins, James C. Enterprise in the Nonprofit Sector. In *The Nonprofit Organization: Essential Readings*, edited by David L. Gies, J. Stevens Ott, and Jay M. Shafritz, 315–327. Pacific Grove, CA: Brooks/Cole, 1990.

Kotler, Philip. *Marketing for Nonprofit Organizations*. Englewood Cliffs, NJ: Prentice Hall, 1982.

U.S. Small Business Administration. Unfair Competition by Nonprofit Organizations with Small Business: An Issue for the 1980s. In *The Nonprofit Organization:*

Essential Readings, edited by David L. Gies, J. Steven Ott, and Jay M. Shafritz, 89–91. Pacific Grove, CA: Brooks/Cole, 1990.

Young, Dennis R. Entrepreneurship and Organizational Change in the Human Services. In *The Nonprofit Organization: Essential Readings,* edited by David L. Gies, J. Steven Ott, and Jay M. Shafritz, 301–314. Pacific Grove, CA: Brooks/Cole, 1990.

CHAPTER 7

Marketing Planning and Programs

The executive director of the Summer City Arts Festival is gearing up for this year's event. He was somewhat disappointed in last year's attendance, which fell below projections. As a result, he hopes to do a better job of getting the word out and enlisting the support of board members and others interested in the festival. This seems overwhelming, as there is a lot to organize and prepare. The executive director sighs wearily and makes a mental note that he should begin thinking about developing the brochures for this year's festival.

The executive director of this organization is not alone in feeling overwhelmed and confused when approaching the task of marketing a program, service, event, or organization. An effective marketing program is not the result of a single inspiration or the efforts of dedicated people alone. Like all administrative functions, effective marketing requires planning and organization.

Larger corporations, both nonprofit and for-profit, may have the resources to maintain marketing departments filled with individuals who have specific skills and expertise and are committed fully to various aspects of marketing. Often, smaller organizations lack the resources to add positions dedicated exclusively to marketing, and the marketing task falls upon the shoulders of one or more individuals within the organization who are already busy doing other things. Under these conditions, marketing may be last on the list of organizational priorities, and a marketing program is carried out poorly if at all.

THE EVOLUTION OF MARKETING PROGRAMS

Few organizations move directly to an effective, efficient marketing program from having no program at all. Almost always, there is an evolutionary process that takes place as the organization begins to recognize the need for a marketing program and build it gradually, piece by piece. Several stages might be identified in the construction of marketing programs:

• **Marketing denial**—many nonprofits still resist the concept of marketing altogether. They may deny the competitive nature of the nonprofit marketplace and cite the lack of a budget for experimenting with innovations, or lack the knowledge to carry forth a marketing program. In addition, the organization may see its offerings as inherently worthwhile and therefore not in need of marketing.

• **Haphazard marketing**—the organization lacks any sense of organization in its marketing efforts at this stage. Marketing may be exclusively communications oriented, with elements such as the production of brochures, public service announcements, and the development of a speakers' bureau forming the core of the marketing program. At this point, however, such efforts are not coordinated or integrated.

• **Budget-driven marketing planning**—often, nonprofits are forced to do minimal planning for marketing activities at budget preparation time. Each program or the organization as a whole may need to have an annual budget prepared that includes an estimate for marketing costs. The leadership of the organization may develop a rough guess as to what the year's marketing activities will be and what they will cost.

• **Program-specific marketing planning**—due to the nature of some programs and/or the people who run them, specific programs may develop marketing plans that will vary in their scope and effectiveness. New projects or those that carry high risk or expenditures may be the targets for the introduction of a marketing orientation, although at this point they are not integrated with other efforts within the organization.

• **Short-term marketing planning**—the organization that is beginning to make a serious effort to institute a marketing program may develop short-term plans, addressing a period of one year or less. At this stage limited efforts at organizational integration may be made, because there is some comprehensive sense of the organization's overall marketing goals and activities for the year.

• **Long-term marketing planning**—an organization may, over time, begin to look at marketing and administrative tasks as long-term propositions. Not only does the organization seek to achieve good results this year, but it seeks to position itself favorably over the long haul. At this point the organization may look at long-term activities that will help achieve success in the marketplace.

• **Strategic marketing planning**—this is the highest level of marketing integration and planning to which an organization can aspire. The organization has set overall strategic goals and has determined its ideal position in the marketplace. Marketing efforts tend to be organization wide, with a sense of direction and long-term commitment to the organization and its destiny.

WHO IS A NONPROFIT MARKETER?

An organization that lacks the resources to hire a dedicated marketer or create a marketing department may choose not to explore opportunities to develop a marketing program, which is unfortunate. Perhaps even more unfortunate, however, is the fact that organizations that do have specialized marketing professionals tend to believe that it is the "job" of these individuals to "do the marketing" for the organization. In fact, marketing, when done effectively, is a total organizational effort, with marketing specialists serving to support, guide, and oversee the program.

Marketing, in fact, is everyone's job. Like most successful organizational initiatives, marketing should have the attention and support of top management and the board of directors and should support strategic goals and priorities set at that level. In this sense, marketing is a top-down activity. Effective marketing can and should flow from the bottom up as well. Those in the "front lines" will have a valuable perspective on the organization and the wants and needs of those it exists to serve. A partnership of individuals at all levels of the organization represents the ideal, with the entire nonprofit sensitized to the issue of marketing and routine transactions viewed as opportunities to carry out the organization's marketing objectives.

There are a variety of approaches and structures that can work and are needed within the nonprofit organization, depending upon the mission, size, and scope of the organization.

Involve the Board

Nonprofits must rely on the board of directors for support and assistance with their efforts. In some cases, the board's contribution simply will be to rubber-stamp a budget or authorize creating a position to develop a marketing orientation within the organization. In other cases, the board members become direct marketers themselves. At times, nonprofits recruit board members for their marketing expertise so that they can utilize these skills when they cannot afford to hire. The board can help by using their contacts to approach individuals or organizations that may provide funds, corporate partnerships, or other resources. Grassroots organizations may enlist board members in the "nitty-gritty" work of addressing envelopes and delivering posters. In any case, the board ultimately is responsible for the success of the organization and therefore should attend to the marketing efforts and consider them a vital ingredient of that success. However, board efforts must be focused and their work integrated with staff efforts in order to avoid a runaway marketing program led by powerful, well-intentioned but ineffective board volunteers.

Involve the Top Management

The role of the top management in the marketing organization will vary, depending upon the structure and complexity of the organization and the talents and interests of those in charge. However, without commitment from the top, the development of an effective marketing program is unlikely. The CEO of the organization or a designee should be responsible for the development of a marketing program; ideally the commitment to a market-driven organization will be set at the top, with the spirit and the mandate reaching those below. Management should be knowledgeable and able to provide competent leadership in marketing, which involves a body of knowledge and a set of skills with which not all managers are endowed.

Hire a Marketer

As mentioned previously, hiring a marketer should not be viewed as a panacea. If a marketing position or department is in place, the support and involvement of the board, top management, and other staff at all levels remains crucial. The marketer must be knowledgeable not only in the theory and practice of marketing but also must know and understand the nonprofit organization and its commitments to mission and its constituencies. The organization should have a clear idea of its expectations and the structure it plans to put in place prior to creating a marketing function.

Form a Marketing Committee

A marketing committee can be a useful tool in an organization in conjunction with or as a substitute for a marketing professional or department. Often, a multidisciplinary committee can represent a helpful forum for organizing and implementing an organization-wide marketing approach. A marketing committee must be chaired and directed by competent leadership and must work together to look at the "big picture" in the organization. Often, such groups will require some education and guidance from someone who is a skilled marketer.

Utilize Volunteer Resources

Volunteers can be useful in planning and implementing every stage of a marketing program. If properly supervised and utilized, they can make a marketing program affordable and possible for an organization that otherwise lacks resources. Sometimes, for-profit businesses corporations will "loan" professional expertise to nonprofits, and senior volunteer organizations provide retired marketing executives. Even volunteers with little or no marketing expertise can implement the nuts and bolts of a marketing program if they are well supervised and trained.

Hire a Consultant

Consultants can provide focused, specific expertise to an organization on a short-term or project-specific basis without making a permanent commitment to an employee who must be added to the payroll. However, a consultant can represent a financial drain on the organization because of high fees, and if expectations are not made clear, the organization can waste precious resources in pursuing activities or approaches not compatible with organizational goals. A consultant who singlehandedly develops plans or programs, however technically brilliant, actually can prove destructive to the organization by breeding suspicion, hostility, and lack of cooperation in those within the organization who were excluded from the process.

Integrate Marketing with Other Existing Functions

There are many organizations that develop effective marketing programs by integrating them with other functions. Department or division heads can develop a marketing program, or it can be added to functions such as program planning and evaluation or public relations, if those are already in place. The organization must see that those responsible understand their new undertaking and that training and information on marketing is made available to the uninitiated. In addition, marketing responsibilities must be emphasized so they do not find a place on the back burner, bumped aside from other, more familiar and "pressing" duties.

Clearly, there are many ways an organization can construct a marketing structure, and it may be ot some benefit to combine several of the elements mentioned above. Regardless of the structure, the organization will need to build a corporate culture that emphasizes that marketing is compatible with and supports the organization's overall mission.

THE IMPORTANCE OF MARKETING PLANS

Regardless of the marketing structure an organization chooses to implement, there should be a carefully thought out and developed plan that provides the blueprint for organizational activities. A marketing plan is a document that reflects the marketing planning process and ideally should include many of the marketing activities described in this book.

Many organizations attempt to accomplish complex tasks in fulfillment of their mission and in the interests of their growth and survival, and they need to focus their marketing efforts in order to best accomplish this task:

The National Organization for Human Harmony (NOHH) is developing a number of programs that will promote understanding and unity among individuals of different races, nationalities, and religious backgrounds. In some cases, the organization sees its market falling into natural segments along those lines. At this point, NOHH is attempting to market both its multicultural programs and its message of peace and harmony among people of all backgrounds. Clearly, there are many ways NOHH can approach these markets, by designing offerings that will promote its mission and by working to provide public information. Because they have a small staff but a national focus, NOHH is in need of an organized effort in its marketing program.

A marketing plan can help an organization such as this one define what it is attempting to accomplish and can provide structure to its efforts so that resources are not expended in a haphazard manner.

Marketing plans can be developed from several viewpoints:

• A marketing plan can be geared toward the organization as a whole, in which overall strategies for a small organization or integrated strategies for the components of a larger one are presented.

• It can be program or offering specific, in which case a plan for one specific area such as the food distribution function of a hunger program or the counseling programs of a hospice are addressed.

• The plan also can be market specific, addressing the organization's marketing efforts geared at one market or market segment; examples might include a marketing plan for all services geared toward low-income mothers in a community health center or a marketing plan to address the needs of children in a program for the homeless.

In any case, the marketing plan should address the **4 Ps of marketing:**

• What the product is and how it fits into the marketplace
• How the offering will be priced or paid for
• The place or method of distributing or delivering the program, product, or service
• The promotion or sales strategies that will carry the message and bring about the desired result in terms of utilization, awareness, or change

DEVELOPING A MARKETING PLAN

As with nearly all other administrative functions, there is no single right way to prepare a marketing plan. The format and presentation will depend upon the scope and complexity of the nonprofit and on whether the plan addresses one or more individual programs or the organization as a whole. Ideally, the organization should have a marketing plan for each program or segment of its business, whether new or existing.

This will provide both a prospective look at the course of action to be taken and a yardstick against which to measure the organization's progress.

The nonprofit, especially the smaller organization, should avoid both ends of the spectrum of planning complexity. Neither overkill efforts that produce gorgeous planning documents no one will read nor scanty, poorly developed and defined plans will prove to be an effective use of the organization's time and money. The following guidelines address some of the typical ingredients of a marketing plan.

Executive Summary

Although the first section of a typical plan will be the executive summary, this generally should be written last. The executive summary is what it sounds like—a brief summary of the proposal aimed at the executive who is too busy to be concerned with the details of the plan. However, this section of the plan also may be of interest to the board, managers, and others who have a stake in the organization and how it positions itself. The executive summary should be brief, readable, and give a good overview of what is proposed.

Introduction and Background

The marketing plan should address trends in the environment, local, regional, and national, that relate to the program at hand. Clearly, all offerings should be developed in response to the wants and/or needs of the target group(s) of the organization. The marketing plan should justify the offerings and include a presentation of or reference to objective data. The background section also might include information on the organization and its evolution. The function of this section is to clearly explain why the project exists or has been proposed and why it will be useful.

Project Description

The project and the resources needed to conduct it should be fully described in this section, by explaining how the wants and/or needs identified above will be provided for by this organization. The project description should address the details of the operation, including the personnel and other resource needs that are essential to its operations. This section forces the marketing planner to explore the actual or potential benefit of the offering and the resource expenditures associated with it.

Situation Analysis

The situation analysis might include all internal and external data and the findings of the SWOT analysis. This represents relevant findings in areas such as the marketplace and external environment, consumer characteristics, competitive profiles, and conclusions reached through market research.

Objective and Strategy Development

This section represents the guts of the marketing plan. It clearly identifies what the organization hopes to accomplish according to a variety of criteria, for example:

- **Mission**—the strategy should relate to the mission of the organization, so the plan is clearly tied to the organization's effectiveness in reaching goals defined in its mission statement.

- **Market share**—boosting the organization's market share or market penetration may be a major goal. If so, it should be apparent how the plan will assist the organization increase the market share.

- **Revenue**—if revenue enhancement is a goal, either through earning or raising additional dollars, the marketing plan should demonstrate how the proposed programs or tactics will lead to an improvement in the revenue base.

A clear statement of strategy is a vital ingredient within the marketing plan. Strategic statements might include the following:

- By adding the support groups detailed in this plan, Services to Families seeks to provide the most comprehensive services to stepfamilies in the state, allowing us to provide excellent service as well as positioning the program to serve as a model and receive regional or national attention.

- Scholarships for Stars plans to undertake a major promotional campaign to publicize its activities in providing college information and funding to exceptional students from low-income neighborhoods. This publicity is geared to increasing awareness and name recognition in preparation for a major fund-raising drive.

An organization should be able to state what it plans to do and why. Ideally, this should be related to the organization's overall strategy, and the marketing plan should support the strategic plan.

Specific Marketing Goals and Objectives

Earlier, we discussed the importance of setting goals and objectives as a part of the strategic planning effort. Let's review the definition of goals and objectives:

- A goal is a statement that describes an intent or desired outcome in broad terms. It tells what the organization is trying to accomplish. Marketing goals ideally should flow from the organization's strategic plan and should define the overall position the organization hopes to achieve.

- Objectives tell what the organization specifically proposes to do in order to reach the goals it has set. Accompanied by specific, measurable action plans, these objectives will help define the course the organization plans to take in order to achieve its goals.

Marketing goals, objectives, and action plans form the basis for the implementation and control of the plan as a whole and therefore will need to spell out what the organization plans to do and how that should be accomplished.

Marketing Budget

Nonprofit marketing budgets can range from nothing to megabucks, depending on the organization's size, scope, mission, and the availability of resources. Ideally, budgets for all functions are developed as the result of a planning process, wherein priorities, activities, and their costs are identified. If marketing plans are developed on a service or department basis, they can easily form the basis for the determination of an aggregate organizational marketing budget. The total budget can be developed simply by adding departmental figures, supplemented by whatever marketing activities will be conducted on the corporate level for the organization as a whole.

The budgeting section of the marketing plan should include all direct marketing costs as well as an estimate of the operating costs of the program. Particularly if the offering is a new one, the full costs of bringing the project to fruition should be considered, including personnel, space, supplies, and other essentials. Listing all projected expenditures of the program will give the organization some sense of the program's operating requirements and will provide criteria against which to measure financial performance.

Volume and revenue projections are equally important. The organization should set, in advance, expectations regarding volume in whatever terms are meaningful, considering the number of units of service, visitors, or items sold. Again, this estimates the organization's market for its services and provides a yardstick against which to measure results and by which to plan for program needs. Revenue projections should include all anticipated financial support, including sources such as direct program revenue, government funds, and philanthropy.

At times, budgeting for "frills" such as marketing is done on the basis of determining what the organization can afford, which often is not much. It is at the budgeting stage that some organizations may be tempted to abandon early ideas and efforts related to marketing the organization.

Implementation and Control

One of the most important and often neglected parts of developing a marketing plan is implementation and control. Often, organizations are so impressed by their foresight and brilliance in planning new directions and ideas that they fail to consider that in many ways the work of the plan begins when the idea is fleshed out and committed to paper.

Specific action plans, time frames, and assignment of responsibility need to be specified in this portion of the plan, because they form the mechanisms by which the plan will become operational. This section of the plan should specify concrete actions and indicate how, when, and by whom the implementation of the plan is to be monitored. Without adequate followup, the organization will be unable to determine whether their ideas were in fact brilliant and lack information needed to make a mid-course correction if needed.

Appendices and Exhibits

Often, there is some value in adding background or supplemental information to the body of a marketing plan. For example, a detailed demographic report or the results of a market research project might be added to this section of a report. The point is to provide documentation and show that the organization has done its homework without cluttering up the body of the document with extraneous materials that make it complex and difficult to read. Sad to say, many of those to whom a detailed plan is circulated will fail to read it at all, and others will scan the document. Even those who read the body of the document in earnest will appreciate having supporting data placed at the end where it can be referred to as needed.

FEASIBILITY STUDIES

Along with the use of criteria for new ventures such as those mentioned in the last chapter, any organization that is seriously contemplating a major new idea or program should conduct a **feasibility study,** which is similar to and can be a precursor to the development of a marketing plan. A new idea that is subjected to such scrutiny has a better chance of survival, as the process will help to screen out unfavorable concepts and identify pitfalls prior to startup.

The purpose of a feasibility study is to separate a "good" idea from a "bad" one and to lend some objectivity to a decision-making process that is too often subjective in nature. If the organization has a general direction it intends to pursue, identified in a strategic planning process, this can provide the framework for the feasibility study. The study will help to answer questions such as:

- Does this idea fit with our overall goals and mission?
- Is there a market for the service? Is there a sufficiently large group of individuals whose wants and needs would be served by this idea?
- Is there funding available from program revenues, government monies, philanthropy, or other sources?
- Are there actual or potential competitors who might make this idea less feasible?
- Do we have the scope, personnel, and general skills to make this idea happen?

By following the general guidelines for a marketing plan outlined above and answering questions such as these, the organization can study an idea in advance of implementing it. The conclusions of a feasibility study might fall into four general categories:

1. **Proceed with the idea.** If the proposed new line of business receives a favorable report in the feasibility study, the organization may choose to move toward the implementation of the idea. This, of course, is the ideal outcome of such a study, as the originator(s) of the idea receive satisfaction from a job well done and the organization benefits from a potential rising star among its offerings. However, conducting a feasibility study in order to provide rubber stamp approval to a decision that has already been made is all too common and clearly will yield few substantial benefits.

2. **Start with a pilot project.** If the conclusions of the feasibility study indicate a questionable future for an idea that still appears to hold merit or organizational resources limit present capacity to take risks, an alternative is to proceed with a scaled-down version of the original concept. Although this will require less organizational commitment, and therefore less risk, it also may reduce the chance of success for the new offering. An attractive idea watered down in this fashion may lose some of its luster as it moves toward the marketplace.

3. **Proceed with a revision of the original concept.** Often, an objective feasibility study will identify one or more flaws in the original idea—perhaps the program will lose too much money, require facilities that are impractical to acquire, or come up against regulations that will make implementation a nightmare. There may be alternatives or variations on the original theme that will preserve some of the benefits and minimize the drawbacks of proceeding with the idea. This type of creative juggling can help the organization salvage worthwhile offerings.

4. **Scrap the idea.** There is no shame in determining that an idea is fatally flawed. In fact, if every idea or proposal is implemented, it is either a sign of exceptional genius or exceptional stupidity on the part of that organization. Upon closer scrutiny, the organization may determine that the original idea has more drawbacks than advantages or that the drawbacks are of sufficient magnitude to warrant rejecting the idea. However, this year's loser may be next year's superstar, so the organization should be on the lookout for ideas that although impractical today can be reconsidered in the future in light of a changing environment.

MARKET AUDIT AND PROGRAM EVALUATION

Following the development of a marketing plan, a **market audit** can be an important ongoing element of an organization's marketing program. It involves a periodic look at where the organization is now, and how successful it has been in reaching its goals. The market audit might include:

- An examination of products and services and their continued relevance to the mission
- An evaluation of the effectiveness of those products and services in working toward their stated goals
- An examination of new industry trends or market segments the organization must address
- The organization's strategy in addressing the 4 Ps of marketing

As discussed earlier in this book, every effective organization should continually examine the external environment as well as internal operations in order to ensure that it is optimally marketing the organization by:

- Identifying what is wanted and needed
- Bringing an individual or group that has wants or needs

together with an individual or group that can satisfy those
wants or needs

- Focusing on understanding and serving the client, customer,
  or consumer.

This audit clearly bears a strong resemblance to the feasibility study
described above. No idea is guaranteed permanent feasibility on the
merit of once having gained such designation. The organization must
continually ask itself, "If we weren't already in this business, would we
enter it today?" If the answer is no, the organization may need to seriously examine one or more of its offerings to determine whether there
is any justification in continuing. As in the feasibility study, there are
several possible conclusions that might be reached from a marketing
audit:

Continue the offering unchanged. If the program or service is found
to be of continual benefit to the organization, the recommendation
may be to leave it alone and support its continued success.

Institute refinements or revisions in the offering. Organizational
offerings may not be terminally ill but may be in need of
attention. Making changes in elements, such as the way the
program is promoted, the market segment(s) toward which it
is aimed, or the hours of operation, may restore the program
to health. Alternatively, perhaps the need was overestimated or
has dwindled since the program's inception, and the offering
may be more successful if it is scaled back. If the program is
not periodically reexamined, refinements such as these may be
missed, and the program may be hastened along to the decline
stage of the product life cycle.

Eliminate the program. Practical realities dictate that it is time to
"pull the plug" on an offering that might have been successful at
one time. In cases such as this, organizational as well as individual
sentiments can cloud objectivity and judgment. However, a mark
of a healthy organization is its willingness to change and adapt to
the realities it faces as it moves toward an uncertain future.

The audit, then, can be considered the final step in the marketing planning process. It is no accident, however, that it bears a strong resemblance to the earlier steps presented in this book. Marketing clearly is a
cycle, with no well-defined beginning, middle, or end. There is no starting or stopping a marketing approach within the effective nonprofit
organization; it simply is a matter of continual refinement and an ongoing
approach to the management of the organization.

REVIEW QUESTIONS

1. A typical organization might move through several stages in the evolution and development of its marketing program. Describe these stages.
2. Who are some of the key players in the development and implementation of a marketing program?
3. What are some of the advantages and disadvantages of various marketing structures within the nonprofit organization?
4. Why is a marketing plan necessary in order to have an effective, market-driven organization?
5. What is the difference between a program-specific and a market-specific marketing plan?
6. What are some of the major sections of the typical marketing plan, and what are their functions?
7. What are marketing goals and objectives, and why should they be formulated?
8. What is meant by "implementation and control" in regard to a marketing plan? Why is it important?
9. What is a feasibility study, and what role does it play in examining the market for and structure of a new offering?
10. What is the market audit? Why could it be considered both the end and the beginning of the marketing planning process?

MINI CASE STUDY

The American Association for Pancreatic Illness is an organization that concerns itself with the treatment, research, and education of diseases of the pancreas. The organization deals with several distinct groups of individuals in carrying out its mission, including medical researchers, physicians, other health professionals, patients, and their significant others. It also must attract resources through its fund raising program and allocate those resources to research, education, support, and treatment activities.

The association recognizes the complexity of marketing so many aspects of the organization to so many different constituencies and is interested in developing an integrated, efficient way of marketing its program and services.

1. How might this organization approach the development of a marketing plan?
2. What are some of the key issues that should be addressed in such a plan?

3. What elements might be included in the development of strategies, goals, and objectives for this organization?

FURTHER READING

Barry, Bryan W. *Strategic Planning Workbook for Nonprofit Organizations*. St. Paul, MN: Amherst H. Wilder Foundation, 1986.

Espy, Siri N. *Handbook of Strategic Planning for Nonprofit Organizations*. New York: Praeger Publishers, 1986.

Kotler, Philip. *Principles of Marketing*. Englewood Cliffs, NJ: Prentice-Hall, 1986.

CHAPTER 8

Marketing Communications

Assistance to Victims of Crime was founded ten years ago as an organization which would work with those who have experienced violent assaults. A sad reflection of our times, the crime rate has risen and so has the need for the assistance center. The organization has developed specialized units to deal with victims of rape, assault, and robbery and a program for the families of murder victims. As the marketing committee contemplates its task for the next several years, it is aware of the need to continue to foster and improve relationships with law enforcement agencies, but also wants to take its message public, especially addressing frequently underreported crimes such as rape and domestic violence and encouraging victims to seek assistance.

Effective communication is a vital ingredient of success in every nonprofit organization. Without the ability to "get the word out," the organization would have no board, staff, volunteers, clients, or funds. Every organization faces the task of communicating with a diverse group of people on many subjects and should realize that its life depends on its effectiveness in doing so.

Marketing, as we discussed in the first chapter, is not synonymous with communication, promotion, and advertising, and it is no accident that marketing communication is addressed here after the topics of strategic planning, market research, and segmenting and targeting the market. To be carried out effectively, the organization's communications program should be a logical outgrowth of earlier decisions and should serve to publicize strategically chosen and targeted offerings. Unfortunately, many organizations hold a narrow, short-term view of advertising and promotion, failing to recognize that all communications should be an integrated part of the organization's strategy for success.

WHY DO NONPROFITS COMMUNICATE?

There are, within many organizations, diehard souls who believe that nonprofit organizations should not engage in anything called marketing or advertising. However, without marketing and some form of marketing communications it is difficult to imagine that any nonprofit would be able to carry out its mission effectively. Let's flash back to our definition of marketing:

- **A means of identifying what is wanted and needed**
- **A mechanism for bringing an individual or group that has**

wants or needs together with an individual or group that
can satisfy those wants or needs
- **A focus on understanding and serving the client, customer,
or consumer.**

Clearly, marketing communications provides the mechanism for bringing together consumers with providers, corresponding with the second
part of our definition above. The organization relies on the accurate,
favorable flow of information in order to accomplish its goals.

Marketing communication can accomplish a number of marketing
tasks, including:

- Helping to identify the organization to the public
- Creating awareness of the organization in the community
  and the organization's target group(s)
- Developing a comprehension of the organization and its work
- Arousing interest in the organization and its offerings
- Keeping the organization in the mind of important groups
  via a steady stream of communications over time

It would be extremely difficult to find a nonprofit that does not have
needs. Even if the organization has too many clients, adequate funding,
and a positive image, it may need volunteers or new blood on its board.
Even in the unlikely event that an organization has all its current needs
completely satisfied, it must work to maintain that fortunate circum-
stance. Developing and carrying forward an effective communications
program can help the organization position itself for continued future
success.

WHAT DO NONPROFITS COMMUNICATE?

Simply communicating is not enough; the organization can all too
easily communicate the wrong message. Exactly what the organization
wishes to communicate is one of the first decisions in any marketing
communications effort.

There are two levels of communication that carry messages about
the organization:

- **Formal** communication takes the form of official, planned efforts,
such as press releases, brochures, or advertising. It carries the approved
message of the organization, generally through predetermined channels.

- **Informal** communication is the flow of information, impressions,
or images out of the organization through a number of exchanges that
may be unplanned and spontaneous, such as the staffer's conversation

with a friend about what really goes on at work or a consumer's encounter with a maintenance worker who is repairing a water fountain.

Often, the informal channel is as powerful a determiner of the organization's image as formal communications, especially in the case of a small, grassroots community organization. In approaching both levels of communication, one of the first decisions made in any organization should be to strategically determine exactly what it wishes to communicate.

There may be specific factual information that the organization needs to disseminate—the opening of a new program, an upcoming special event, or ten reasons to stop smoking are examples. In this case, the communication is geared toward getting that specific message across to those individuals the organization has targeted. Communication, however, is more than simply conveying facts to a designated audience.

Communication, ideally, will focus on building and maintaining an image in the community or the region or the nation, depending upon the geographic reach of the organization. It is a strategic issue to determine what that image should be. Naturally, the organization will want a "positive" image, but that can take many forms. The organization may wish to be perceived as friendly, businesslike, compassionate, fun, exciting, comforting, helpful, or accessible.

Obviously, not all these images will be appropriate for each nonprofit. A center that provides grief counseling will seek an image of compassion and healing rather than fun and excitement, but a children's museum would be delighted with an aura of merriment and exploration. The image projected will depend in large part on the types of people the organization is attempting to reach and should be geared to creating a positive impression. This conclusion concerning image should form the cornerstone of all marketing communications efforts. The organization's image should be consistent, reflecting an effort over time to build a desired reputation. Whatever the organization's mission, certain elements such as caring, quality, and concern about the consumer should always be present and should be reflected in all levels of the organization as well as in all communications.

One way organizations seek recognition is through the use of a logo. Although a logo is not essential for the operation of a nonprofit organization, the appearance of communication pieces is important. They should be consistent, using the same "signature" whether it be an actual logo or simply the way the name is printed or the color of the stationery. Over a period of time, the organization's target groups should be able to recognize the organization's communications much as consumers know a Campbell's soup can or a Cheerios box. This is all part of building the nonprofit's image.

WHO IS A MARKETING COMMUNICATOR?

Although it is tempting to equate marketing communications with advertising, publicity, and other traditional tools, it is important for the organization to recognize that all communication that flows into, out of, and within the organization represents a marketing opportunity. From the CEO to the janitor, all personnel within the organization represent it and its interests to the public. An organization that develops an expensive advertising campaign but tolerates a rude receptionist may be wasting its dollars, and a history of favorable publicity can be wiped out instantly if a staff member is found to be abusing clients. Looking within before placing emphasis on external communications can be a worthwhile endeavor.

Many organizations have created a specialized marketing communications function, often designated as or merged with public or community relations. However, there are a variety of ways that the organization can utilize the available human resources to enhance its marketing communications efforts.

Some organizations have successfully enlisted celebrity spokespersons. Due to a quirk in human nature, much of the public the organization strives to reach may be impressed by a familiar, famous face. Although the celebrity may have no specialized knowledge in the field, the increased attention and credibility associated with the use of well-known individuals can bring much desired publicity to the nonprofit.

There also are ways that nonprofit organizations can realize the benefit of marketing communications expertise at little or no cost. Media personalities or professionals are often targeted for board membership in order to gain their support and expertise. Some communications firms may be willing to do a limited amount of work free of charge, or *pro bono*. Individual professionals, both retired and active in the field, may volunteer their assistance. Colleges and universities also may be sources of expertise, as students on the undergraduate and graduate level may adopt the organization as a learning laboratory of sorts.

The truly marketing-oriented organization will work from within to control and enhance its communication efforts and will look outside to the community to develop additional resources with which it can build a communications network. The enterprising organization can communicate quite effectively with the public without breaking its budget.

WITH WHOM DO NONPROFITS COMMUNICATE?

We discussed earlier in this book the many groups with which the nonprofit organization must do business in order to exist and fulfill its mission. Diverse groups such as consumers, corporations, foundations, individual donors, government funders, volunteers, board members, referral agents, significant others, stakeholders, and employees are all vital to the life of the nonprofit and are potential targets for marketing communication efforts. For example:

- Consumers of a home-delivered meal service for the elderly receive holiday greetings from the agency.
- Corporations and foundations are sent invitations to an open house.
- Individual donors get a letter of thanks that details the good work made possible by their generosity.
- Government funders are given periodic reports on the organization's activities.
- Volunteers are invited to an annual recognition event at which they are awarded a certificate for service.
- Board members are asked to donate their time to the work of the organization.
- Referral agents are targeted for receiving a brochure describing a new service that may be of interest.
- Significant others of those in cancer support groups are asked to attend a special program for families.
- Stakeholders are asked to write to their representative regarding pending legislation that would adversely affect the organization.
- Employees receive the quarterly newsletter highlighting the organization's accomplishments and the important role they have played in this progress.

Clearly, these groups are all vital to the continued health of the organization and are worthy of communication to gain and maintain their support. Each group, however, may have somewhat different interests, and different appeals will be needed in order to gain the desired response. Communicating the wrong message in the wrong way can prove quite damaging. The communications task for the nonprofit organization obviously is quite complex.

LINKING COMMUNICATIONS TO SEGMENTED AND TARGETED GROUPS

If the organization has conducted a thorough analysis of the groups mentioned above that are vital to its success, its communication task will be a great deal easier. For communications to be successful, it is important that the message be appropriate to those who are the intended recipients.

The nonprofit may choose to target a particular communication to the market as a whole or to specific segments. This decision may depend partly on the organization's resources, as it can be quite expensive and time consuming to develop separate promotional pieces for all groups and subgroups involved with the organization, for example:

> A hospice has a number of important groups with which it must communicate. The patient and the family are interested in the type of service available and how it will meet their needs; referral agents at local healthcare organizations want to know how the hospice will help their patients and how referrals are made; and potential donors need to be convinced of the worthiness of the cause and to see how their dollars will help. Even if we target only these three groups for communication efforts, we can see that three separate approaches are needed in order to achieve the desired results: (1) an opportunity to serve patients and their families, (2) referrals from health care professionals, and (3) sustaining contributions from donors.

An organization that wishes to build an effective communications program must understand the concepts of segmenting and targeting—breaking the market as a whole into meaningful subgroups and selecting certain of these groups as the focus of marketing efforts. Even within a group, such as consumers, there can be a number of subgroups with which the organization must communicate:

> A domestic violence program serves primarily female victims of abuse, who differ in age, education, and psychological and economic capacity to become self-supporting. However, the organization may find that some of its battered clients are male, with somewhat different concerns and issues. In addition, the organization serves children who range in age from infancy to adolescence; obviously, this group can be segmented on age as well as the type of abuse (physical, sexual, or psychological) and its effects (depression, violent behavior, poor performance in school). The program also may serve the offenders who may be male or female, young or old, and motivated by staying out of jail or improving their lives. Communicating with such a diverse maze of groups or subgroups in such a manner that each will feel that the organization has something to offer them can be a difficult challenge, yet the type of appeal that will bring a young woman with three preschoolers to the program will be ineffective for a male offender who is facing arrest.

Through market research, the organization may be able to identify particular attitudes or characteristics in its target group(s) that it must address in its communications in order to effectively reach those individuals. For example, knowledge that a fear of contracting AIDS deters potential blood donors could form an important part of the work of the marketing communicator, who must ensure that the message of safety is disseminated through publicity, advertising, or other means. Or an individual who might deny the possibility of addiction to drugs prescribed by the kindly family doctor might hear the message that overuse of such drugs can cause problems. These are examples of targeting communications to specific groups—fearful blood donors and middle-class prescription drug addicts.

Obviously, the nonprofit must strive to have a good handle on the characteristics of its actual and potential markets before embarking on a communications campaign. Understanding the ways markets can be segmented, such as by demographic, geographic, and psychographic information, will give the marketer many clues as to the content of effective communication. Marketing communication, then, must be strategic if the organization is to get the most bang for its buck. Like the planning of programs and services, the message must be carefully targeted and based on a process that includes both research and deliberate strategy development.

COMMUNICATION STRATEGIES

An organization that understands and uses the concepts of segmenting and targeting can use these tools to focus its communication efforts on the group(s) that they have identified as priority segments of the market. The organization may have several choices in its marketing communication efforts.

Mass Marketing

An organization that engages in mass marketing is attempting to reach all segments of the market through a single communications effort. An ad in a metropolitan newspaper asking for donations or a brochure sent to all households in the organization's service area are examples of mass marketing. Here, the message is in no way tailored to the specific recipient, and a "one size fits all" approach to communications is used. The advantage is that it is much less costly and complex to produce a single message to send to the public at large, and the organization does not engage in the detective work needed to track down targets that meet a particular description. However, a generic message may have less appeal to all segments of the market and may miss the mark in reaching those who might respond to a more personalized, targeted approach.

Concentration on One Market Segment

The organization that concentrates on one market segment may decide to appeal to one type of individual exclusively. An organization that attempts to recruit volunteers in a senior center or attract clients in a business publication is concentrating, for the purposes of that communication, on one specific target group. The advantage is that the communication can be geared to the characteristics and perceived motivations of that group and therefore may be more effective than a general appeal. However, in a sense the organization is "putting all its eggs in one basket" as it narrowly focuses its efforts.

Differentiated Marketing

An organization that has the resources to carry out a differentiated marketing campaign may find that it is effectively able to reach a wide variety of groups. In a differentiated campaign, for example, one message might be sent to wealthy donors, a second to needy clients, and a third to professional agencies which might be involved in the process of providing service. Alternatively, the organization may choose to communicate to specific target consumer groups in different ways, emphasizing the fun of coming to the zoo to children, the economical aspects of the entertainment to parents, and the educational potential to teachers seeking destinations for a field trip. Although it can be complex and expensive and cost-benefit factors should be kept in mind, the organization can reach a wide variety of audiences through efforts at differentiated marketing.

TYPES OF COMMUNICATION

Another strategic decision the organization needs to make is the determination of the **marketing mix**. There are many communications vehicles available, and most organizations will choose to incorporate several into an overall communications plan to form a mix of communication strategies that collectively will reach target groups in an effective, affordable fashion.

Ideally, the organization will develop a communications plan that will cover a span of one or more years. Elements of the plan naturally will follow a calendar of events, taking advantage of such designations as Library Week, Hospital Week, or the organization's anniversary. Other communications may be scheduled around special events such as an annual fund raiser, the scheduled opening of a new program, or the kickoff of a capital campaign. Some communications may occur on a regular basis, such as a quarterly newsletter or an annual report. Such a schedule of events provides the organization with a skeleton of basic communication opportunities and gives it a framework for planning its communications program.

In the course of a nonprofit organization's life, there are a number of forums it may choose to utilize, depending on the message to be sent, budget, and the appropriateness of the vehicle for getting the specific word out. The following section describes some of the ways in which nonprofits communicate.

Advertising

Advertising takes the form of paid messages that promote the organization's ideas, offerings, or the organization itself. It can help the organization reach the masses and carry the message more extensively than many other techniques.

Advertising can be a very expensive undertaking and represents a leap the nonprofit may choose not to take without professional assistance. The advertising effort must catch the eye or ear of its intended audience and must convey sufficient interest and appeal to produce the desired results.

In order to effectively advertise, the organization must make a number of decisions. First, there is the choice of media.

Television advertising can be quite costly and may be out of reach for most smaller nonprofit organizations. **Radio** advertising tends to be more affordable, and **print media** include national, local, and regional newspapers, magazines, and trade journals, so that the expense can vary from astronomical to quite affordable. Obviously, targeting plays a major role in strategic decisions regarding advertising. A program for underprivileged youth will not reach many potential clients in an arts publication, nor will an organization promoting highbrow cultural events have much success on a radio station that specializes in the latest adolescent music.

Casual observation of television advertising leads to the conclusion that it is no accident that diapers and household products are pushed during soap operas, and sporting goods and life insurance companies sponsor football games. This reflects the careful targeting of advertising to specific segments of the market, an exercise that any nonprofit must undertake if considering an advertising campaign. Determining the target group for the advertising effort and the medium most likely to catch the attention of those individuals within the organization's budget is one of the key elements to advertising success.

Other decisions must be made in the planning of an advertising campaign, as well. The timing of advertising can be very important, as people might be likely to donate money for the homeless in the midst of cold winters or be interested in seeking drug and alcohol treatment after the drunken holidays. Many dual-career yuppies may not listen to the radio or watch television during weekday afternoons, so advertising geared toward them should be scheduled when they will be reached.

The issue of message frequency also must be addressed. Many organizations sustain their communications efforts over time and plan media blitzes to build on this recognition by sending repeated messages. Depending on the goals and budget, the organization will need to work out an advertising schedule that meshes with its use of other forms of communication to form an integrated communications plan.

Sales Promotion

The for-profit sector often uses sales promotion, offering special incentives to buy, coupons, or buy-one-get-one-free specials. Variations on these techniques also are utilized by nonprofit organizations:

- Attendance at the museum is free on Mother's Day for any mother accompanied by one or more of her children.
- Animals are available for adoption at a reduced price if a coupon from the local newspaper is presented.
- A healthcare organization provides free blood pressure screenings to residents in its service area.

Although promotions such as these provide services to the community, they also help to publicize the organization and familiarize the public with its offerings. These promotions are intended to encourage potential consumers to patronize the organization, hopefully as the first step in a mutually beneficial relationship.

Publicity and Public Relations

Publicity is unpaid communication that may take the form of radio, television, newspaper, magazine, or other types of information dissemination about the organization. It may be of a general nature, such as the presentation of a feature story on the organization's good works, or it may be tied to specific events, such as a charity ball, volunteer recruitment, or the organization's twenty-fifth anniversary.

Active attempts at publicity can take several forms and use varied strategies:

- An organization can develop a **press kit,** which includes information about the organization and its offerings. This might include items such as brochures, the annual report, a list of major contributors, reprints of articles about the organization, and letters of endorsement by community leaders or national figures. The purpose of a press kit is to inform the media and other important groups of the good works of the organization, presenting it in a favorable light.

- **Press releases** serve to make a specific statement that the organization hopes will be picked up to receive free publicity in the media. Press releases can publicize an event, provide information about the organization, or announce the opening of a new program. Many nonprofits have worked to develop relationships with the media that will facilitate the publication of their press releases.

- **Feature stories** often are the result of deliberate, well-planned efforts on the part of a nonprofit organization. The publicity-oriented nonprofit continually will be alert to human interest stories as they unfold, focusing on unique programs, dedicated volunteers, or clients who have been helped by the organization. Again, ongoing media relationships can be beneficial, as the organization can directly contact editors or reporters with interesting story ideas. Just as the enterprising nonprofit seeks new ideas, the media is grateful for a good story.

- **Provision of expertise** to the media can provide valuable publicity as well as a community service. Staff members can appear on radio and television talk shows, or can write columns or provide experts to be interviewed in the media. This represents a good exchange of expertise for publicity and helps the public become aware of the nonprofit's existence and offerings.

- **Public service announcement** are a valuable tool available to nonprofit organizations. Free air time, usually sixty seconds or less, is offered to the organization to get its message across. The organization can advance an idea (stop smoking, save the environment) or provide information about its programs or services in a radio or TV spot.

- **A speakers' bureau** sponsored by the nonprofit can work with local groups and organizations to carry the message and provide a valuable community service by educating and informing those who listen to the speakers.

Publicity has a number of advantages over paid advertising on the same media, but it has several drawbacks as well.

- It is free to the organization, which is a boon to the severely limited nonprofit budget.
- It may be perceived to carry more credibility than paid advertising, because the story was written by an "unbiased" journalist who is not overtly representing the organization.
- It may receive more attention than advertising, as readers may focus on an interesting feature story while ignoring ads on the same page.

- It is out of the control of the organization. Although great care may be taken to produce advertising that presents exactly the right message, receiving free publicity places the nonprofit at the mercy of the journalist.
- Publicity may be negative in nature and may even take the form of an expose of the organization's dirty laundry. Lawsuits against the organization or allegations of wrongdoing represent the type of publicity every organization dreads.

Many nonprofits have discovered the value of developing a proactive, aggressive media relations program, which will facilitate success in all of the outlets described above. There can be great benefit in being known to the media—members of the press will think of that organization when seeking information or expertise in the field and the organization's efforts to gain publicity are well received by individuals already familiar with its work.

Direct Mail Marketing

Direct mail marketing is carried out by organizations that want to get a complex message across for a reasonable cost. This form of communication involves mailing a letter, brochure, or other piece directly to an individual whom the organization has targeted as a potential consumer, donor, or stakeholder in the organization. Mailing lists may be generated in-house, using lists of past consumers, donors, or those with whom the organization has had some type of significant contact. They also may be purchased from businesses that provide lists of individuals targeted in specific ways, such as members of professional groups, organizations, or those who have dealt with similar organizations in the past. Mailings can be targeted geographically, with all residents served by a specific zip code or carrier route receiving the communication.

Unfortunately, many people feel that they are bombarded by too much "junk mail," and the organization must take steps to help its communication avoid a premature trip to the circular file. With careful targeting and message development, however, direct mail can be quite an effective means of communicating with those the organization wishes to reach.

Telephone Marketing

Many nonprofits have discovered that the telephone is a powerful communication tool when used for the organization's benefit. Telephone marketing, or telemarketing, can take several forms.

Actual or potential consumers are encouraged to contact the organization. Many organizations do business over the telephone and might have consumers contact them for a variety of purposes such as:

- A hospital's physician referral service links a potential patient with one of their physicians.
- A telephone service allows potential attendees to order tickets to a cultural event, using charge cards as payment.
- Hotlines may provide some direct service and encourage the caller to contact the organization for further assistance.
- Callers may be asked to make pledges by telephone as a result of televised appeals.

The organization initiates telephone contact, for example:

- People attending a free concert register for a drawing and later receive a call soliciting a donation or offering the purchase of tickets for future events.
- Patrons or supporters of a cause are targeted to receive telephone calls to solicit their support.
- A telephone directory or list is used to make the public aware of an event or service or to encourage donations.

Telephone marketing can allow the organization to reach a large number of consumers at a relatively low cost, especially if trained volunteers play a major role in the project. A local corporation might donate its phone bank for a one-shot or short-term project, such as a phone-a-thon. If there is an up-to-date list of targeted prospects, this will raise the odds of success of the efforts over that of "cold calling," calls that are made to parties who may be totally unfamiliar with the organization.

As with any form of marketing, telemarketing has its drawbacks. The organization may incur the wrath of that segment of the public that opposes the intrusion into their privacy with telephone soliciting of any type. A commitment made by telephone is not cast in stone, as many pledges are never followed by a check or other desired action.

Descriptions of the Organization and Its Offerings

Many organizations develop brochures, newsletters, slide presentations, films, and videos that tell the story of the organization. These pieces can be quite expensive productions or can be done in-house on a very low budget. In any case, they must appear professional and represent the organization well if they are to be effective.

- **Brochures** describe the organization, its offerings, and other key information. They may be generic and applicable to all those who are interested in learning about the organization or may be specifically targeted to one or more subgroups, such as potential donors or clients of a particular program.

- **Newsletters** can be targeted to a variety of groups, such as consumers, donors, volunteers, or other organizations with which the sender has or wishes to develop a relationship. They typically inform the reader of the progress and accomplishments of the organization and serve to herald new programs or services.

- **Slides, films, and videos** can inform the viewer of the organization, its history, and good works. When done well, such a presentation can be compelling and can help motivate its audience to donate, volunteer, or take an active interest in the cause advanced by the organization.

Personal Contacts

Some nonprofit organizations have realized tangible benefits from employing a paid sales force. These salespersons may call directly on consumers or referral sources or handle booths at trade shows. In some cases, outreach workers serve as a de facto nonprofit sales force, as personal contact is made with the homeless, the mentally ill, or victims of violent crime in an effort to persuade them to take advantage of the organization's services. Staffers with other duties also may call on other agencies who are potential referral sources or on those who have been targeted as donors.

Although the one-to-one approach to selling may be uncomfortable for the uninitiated, it can be very effective in offering a personalized description of the organization and its mission and in persuading the individual to do what is asked, whether that involves joining the board, making a sizeable donation, or participating in an event.

Personal contacts can be successful if the person making the contact is matched with the prospect to be contacted. An individual who is perceived as having something in common with the prospect may be able to make an effective appeal. Sending a representative who went to the same college, has expertise in the same field, or is well known in the community can help the organization to get a "foot in the door," as experienced fund raisers and marketers will attest.

Word of Mouth

Last but hardly least, the essence and image of the organization is communicated daily by a variety of people both within and outside the organization. The board and staff will carry a message to those who know of their affiliation with the organization, and the customers, referral agents, and stakeholders also will influence public perception of the organization.

Unfortunately, this perception can be negative as well as positive. A staff member airing organizational dirty laundry or a dissatisfied customer can do a great deal of damage. It is an interesting quirk of human nature that in many cases people tend to complain about unfavorable experiences more than they praise satisfactory ones. People expect a certain standard in the quality of their contacts with organizations and may be blase when these expectations are met. In any case, a few disgruntled individuals can be problematic, especially if they are influential or have access to channels of communication to spread their negative impression of the organization.

The nonprofit should strive to leave an impression of high quality and caring in every communication exchange with any member of the public, both out of the charitable spirit that should guide the organization and out of concern for market and business success. In some cases, it only takes one episode of positive or negative dealings with the organization to fix an image—an impression that may travel beyond the one individual who holds it.

TYPES OF COMMUNICATION APPEALS

In designing the communication program, the nonprofit may choose to use one of several types of messages. The type of communication should be tailored to the characteristics of those who are targeted to receive the communication. These communication appeals include:

• A **rational appeal** is targeted to communicate to the receiver's thought processes. Rational communication focuses on the facts, such as the superior technology of a hospital, the effects of drugs on an unborn child, or the services offered by a community center.

• An **emotional appeal** will attempt to "grab" the recipient's guilt, compassion, pride, or fear. Communication in this category might describe the effects of child abuse, starvation in foreign lands, and homelessness.

• A **moral appeal** is targeted toward a sense of right and wrong. Issues such as abortion, support for religious causes, and the need to give help to those less fortunate are likely candidates for an emotional appeal.

An organization's communications mix may include elements of several or all three types of messages. For example, an organization that works against drunk drivers may in different communications present the facts about how little alcohol causes impairment, deal with the family's emotional devastation at losing a teenager to drunk driving, and appeal to hosts to remove the keys from a driver who has had too much out of a sense of obligation to society and its safety. Again, the organization must identify its target(s) for the communication and discern what type of appeal is likely to be effective.

DESIRED OUTCOMES OF COMMUNICATION

Marketing communication may accomplish several different results:

• It may seek **cognitive results,** motivating the recipient of the communication to think of a particular concept or situation, such as homelessness or the consequences of drug use. Cognitive results also may take the form of a change in the way one thinks about a particular situation, such as better understanding of the circumstances that lead to homelessness or a higher regard for the local police and the difficult job they perform.

• **Affective results** may be desired, encouraging those who receive the message to change their feelings about issues, such as racial prejudice, abortion, or AIDS.

• **Behavioral results** may be the direct result of communications or may occur after the cognitive and/or affective message has been received and mulled over. Desired behaviors can include writing out a check for a donation, attending an event, or using birth control.

Often, the organization attempts to evoke cognitive or affective responses as a precursor to encouraging a specific behavior, realizing that communication is a complex process that must be sustained over time in order to be effective.

PRETESTING COMMUNICATION EFFORTS

Whatever the communication strategy, even a seemingly good idea can prove ineffective without pretesting. Often, communication efforts are conceived and developed by professionals with a great deal of education and training but with little insight into the reasoning and motivation of the organization's target groups. For this reason, the organization should take a little extra time and effort to test an idea before taking it public.

Earlier in this book, we explored the topic of market research and its applications in the nonprofit. Techniques such as focus groups and surveys can be helpful in giving the organization some insight into how the message is received and why. Especially when the characteristics of the professionals and the intended audience differ significantly, the organization may find that the message it wishes to send is not the one received. There is no substitute for taking the message directly to members of the target group or those who are similar and then determining their reaction.

The communication should get the message across in a friendly, non-threatening manner that encourages the action or reaction that is desired by the communicator. By using the techniques of market research, the organization can glean some valuable information about reactions to their communication before using valuable resources taking it to the public.

MEASURING THE OUTCOMES OF COMMUNICATION

Marketing communication, as we have discussed, can be a very expensive proposition. If it is ineffective there also is an opportunity cost, the time wasted in failing to get the message across and by not encouraging the desired reaction in those receiving the communication. It is important, then, to evaluate the results of the communication.

Although it may seem like a simple matter to determine whether donations increase or utilization skyrockets in response to a communications program, there often are confounding variables that make it difficult to directly attribute success to that communication effort. There could be cyclical or seasonal factors that would cause an upswing in the desired outcomes independent of the communication efforts or there could be a specific event such as a well-publicized death from a disease or a national tragedy that raises awareness and responsiveness to a cause.

The organization, however, should set goals in its marketing plan that can be measured, and communication efforts should be a part of the planning and evaluation effort. Although such measures are imperfect, a number of measurement tools might be used:

- The organization should plan to measure utilization, donations, or other desired outcomes on a continual basis and note whether a communications campaign causes a noticeable uptick.
- Callers or consumers could be surveyed to determine whether they were aware of and influenced by a communication effort.
- A response card could be included in a brochure or mailing in order to measure the interest generated by the communication.
- Tracking donors against a mailing list for an appeal can provide an indication of whether a recent mailing elicits donations.

These and other market research techniques will help the organization determine whether it has achieved success in its communications efforts. If not, refinements can be made so that the communication reaches the intended target and produces the desired result.

REVIEW QUESTIONS

1. What and with whom do nonprofits typically seek to communicate?
2. Who is a nonprofit marketing communicator?
3. How do the concepts of segmenting and targeting relate to the marketing communications effort?
4. What is the difference between mass and differentiated marketing?
5. List some of the major types of marketing communication and the features of each.
6. What types of communication fall under the heading of publicity, and what are the major advantages of publicity for the nonprofit?
7. What are rational, emotional, and moral appeals in communication?
8. What is meant by the affective, cognitive, and behavioral effects of communications?
9. Why should an organization pretest its communications?
10. Why is measurement of the results of the communication effort important, and how can it be accomplished?

MINI CASE STUDY

Partners in Productivity is a program that offers employment training, counseling, and opportunities to the mentally retarded. The organization's mission is to maximize the functioning of the retarded and to assist them in finding productive employment so that they can be self-supporting and independent.

Partners works with local employers to place its clients in businesses, initially under the supervision of work coaches. For those clients who are lower functioning, the organization provides a sheltered-workshop setting in which various services are performed under contract for businesses. Partners also is in the startup phase of developing its own businesses to provide employment for clients, including a hauling and moving business, a residential and industrial cleaning service, and a package delivery business.

As the organization grows in scope and complexity, the staff and board members contemplate its communication needs for the future, wondering what efforts will be needed and how these might best be carried out.

1. Who are some of the important groups to which Partners must target its communication?
2. What types of communication might be appropriate for this organization?
3. How will the organization know if its efforts have been successful?

FURTHER READING

Johnson, Eugene M. Nonprofits Calling: The Many Faces of Telemarketing. *Nonprofit World*, 6(5), September/October 1988, 20–22.

McGowan, Andrew. PSAs—Free But Not Easy! *Nonprofit World*, 8(3), May/June 1990, 19–22.

Ott, Christine M. Nonprofit Communications on a Shoestring: Thriving in the Midst of Crisis. *Nonprofit World*, 8(2), March/April 1990, 28–31.

Pietzner, Cornelius M. Advertising Your Organization. *Nonprofit World*, 4(5), September/October 1986, 22–23.

Rouner, Donna and Carl Camden. Communicate Your Message With Community Resources. *Nonprofit World*, 8(1), January/February 1990, 23–26.

Zappone, Donald J. Increase Your Organization's Public Recognition and Support. *Nonprofit World*, 4(1), January/February 1986, 18–20.

Conclusion

Marketing, as with any management task, is not something that can be laid out comprehensively and neatly in eight easy chapters. There is no magic formula for nonprofits to follow in order to achieve success in the marketplace; in the nonprofit world, there is not even a universal definition of success in the marketplace! Every organization is charged with using its collective imagination and ability to maneuver in the world to build and carry out an effective marketing program. Luckily, nonprofit organizations are blessed with bright and creative leaders who are accustomed to doing more with less and accomplishing a lot with a little.

There are a few key concepts that the reader should glean from this book that are important in any setting:

• **Marketing is a means of identifying what is wanted and needed, a mechanism for bringing an individual or group that has wants or needs together with an individual or group that can satisfy those wants or needs, and it is focused on serving the client, customer, or consumer.** An organization that understands and accepts the principles inherent in this definition will have a solid base from which to build.

• **Marketing is an important part of fulfilling the organizational mission.** Some nonprofits see marketing as a peripheral or extraneous activity. However, savvy managers realize that without understanding and practicing marketing the chances of successfully carrying out the organizational mission diminish. Marketing should support, not conflict with, the mission.

• **The organization should build a marketing orientation, not just a marketing program.** The nonprofit should view every transaction as a marketing opportunity. Whether making executive decisions or mopping the floor, the people involved with the organization carry important messages—be certain that they are the right ones!

• **Strategic planning and marketing planning form a vital partnership.** Without a sound organizational strategy, marketing is a shot in the dark, and without a marketing orientation, strategic planning will be ineffective and incomplete.

• **The organization must identify and understand the wants, needs, and characteristics of its target groups.** Nonprofits must deal with and market to an astonishing and sometimes appalling number and variety of constituencies, such as consumers, board members, employees, volunteers, funders, and other organizations to name a few. The organization should work to determine how these groups will best be satisfied.

• **Effective marketing necessitates a good grasp on what is going on in the world, both inside and outside the organization.** An effective marketing program depends on a thorough understanding of past history, present realities, and trends for the future. It is important to understand the organization's role in the outside world in order to target and focus marketing efforts.

• **A market-driven orientation will not take for granted that what it does is the best it can do.** In a changing world, the nonprofit will need to continually evaluate the effectiveness of its programs and marketing efforts and be prepared to make tough decisions about starting, scrapping, or changing its offerings.

• **An organization that intends to survive must be prepared to deal with innovation and risk.** Part of the art of management is taking risks that are just extreme enough—those that position the organization for the future without excessively endangering its resources. The ability and willingness to change and grow are vital in the nonprofit marketplace.

• **The nonprofit should take good marketing ideas and translate them into concrete, measurable marketing plans.** Simply having good ideas is never enough. The organization also should focus on the nuts and bolts of implementing those ideas by drawing up a marketing plan to guide its efforts.

• **The organization needs to communicate effectively with important groups in order to get the message out.** Even though marketing communications or promotion may be thought of as the essence of marketing, we deliberately deal with it last. Without the steps that we have considered before, the organization will lack a meaningful concept of what it intends to say and to whom—clearly important considerations to take into account before embarking on a challenging and sometimes costly communications campaign.

Nonprofit organizations face interesting and challenging times and increasingly will need to work smarter within the constraints over which they have no control. The effective nonprofit manager stocks a bag of tricks for all occasions. Hopefully, this book has outlined some concepts, tools, and guidelines that will add to that set of strategies and help the organization push onward.

Index